King Ba

Wole Soyinka was born in
educated at Government Colle
England's Leeds University, and worked in British theatre
before returning to Nigeria in 1960. His earlier prose works
include *The Interpreters*, which was awarded the Jock Campbell
Prize for Commonwealth Literature. Wole Soyinka received
a New Statesman John Whiting Award for 1966–7 and was
Overseas Fellow at Churchill College, Cambridge, in
1973–4, where he wrote the widely acclaimed *Death and the
King's Horseman*. He has been awarded the George Benson
Medal of the Royal Society for Literature and the UNESCO
Medal for the Arts. In 1986 he became the first African writer
to win the Nobel Prize for Literature. Forced into exile in
1994 by military dictatorship, he returned home four years
later and now divides his time between Nigeria and overseas
universities.

King Baabu

(a play in the manner – *roughly* – of Alfred Jarry)

Wole Soyinka

Methuen Drama

Published by Methuen 2002

1 3 5 7 9 10 8 6 4 2

Methuen Publishing Limited,
215 Vauxhall Bridge Road, London SW1V 1EJ

Methuen Publishing Limited Reg. No. 3543167

ISBN 0 413 77175 X

Typeset by SX Composing DTP, Rayleigh, Essex
Printed and bound in Great Britain by
Cox & Wyman Ltd, Reading, Berkshire

King Baabu

Characters

Basha Bash, later, **King Baabu**
Maariya, his wife
Fatasimu, Basha's orderly
General Potipoo, head of the Supreme Council for Advance Redemption, SCAR
Rout, representative of the Recognized and Organized Union of all Trades
Dope, representative of the Divine Order of Prelates Ecumenical
Rent, representative of the Royal Estates Nominal and Traditional
Tikim, officer, brother to Maariya
Shoki ⎱ officers of the Guatuna Army and members of
Kpoki ⎰ SCAR
Commander Bhieu, head of the Rapid Disposal Corps
Chief of Police
Officer
Tutor, later, **Tutor-Motivator**
Attorney-General
Biibabae, son of Baabu and Maariya
Spokesman for the **Bankers**
Chief Justice of Guatuna
Chairman of Mid-East Bank
Oriental Mystic
Marabout
Other Priests
Potiplum ⎱ soldiers, sons of General Potipoo
Potiplan ⎰
Mayor of Batwere
Baabu's Spies, **Women Prisoners**, **Citizens of Batwere**, **Soldiers**, **Crowd**, etc.

King Baabu premiered at the National Arts Theatre, Lagos, on 6 August 2001.

The cast was as follows:

Basha Bash	Yomi Michaels
Maariya	Susan Aderin
Fatasimu	Ayo Lijadu
General Potipoo	Charles Ukpong
Rout	Marcia Hewitt
Dope	Makinde Adeniran
Rent	Wale Ogunyemi
Tikim	Tunji Oyelana
Shoki	Tosan Edremoda-Ugbeye
Kpoki	Victor Eze
Commander Bhieu	Bassey Okon Esanetok
Chief of Police	Kehinde Adeyemo
Officer	Ombo Gogo Ombo
Tutor (*later* **Tutor-Motivator**)	Anthony Ofoegbu
Attorney-General	Bassey Okon Esanetok
Biibabae (*son of* **Baabu** *and* **Maariya**)	Marcia Hewitt
Bankers	Victor Eze, Marcia Hewitt, Ayo Lijadu, Anthony Ofoegbu, Charles Ukpong
Oriental Mystic	Kehinde Adeyemo
Marabout	Tosan Edremoda-Ugbeye
Potiplum	Tunji Sotimirin
Mayor of Batwere	Ombo Gogo Ombo

Baabu's Spies, **Women Prisoners**, **Citizens of Batwere**, **Soldiers**, **Crowd**, etc., were played by members of the cast.

Director Wole Soyinka
Designer Karin Süss
Lighting Designer Anita Vetterli

Act One

Scene One

A broad verandah in front of the former residence of General Uzi, lately deceased. Military personnel, in various stages of undress and casual fatigues – T-shirts over khaki pants, military boots and booties, sneakers and sandals, etc., several with arms slung over their shoulders and dripping with grenades, rocket launchers, and other lethal toys, are moving furniture. Odd-shaped wrapped-up boxes and packages will serve – in and out and in all directions, under the occasional direction of **Lady Maariya**, *the beloved wife of* **Basha Bash**. *The soldiers move about their business oblivious to the exchanges between* **Basha Bash** *and* **Lady Maariya** *who are engaged in their favourite occupation – amorous dialogue.*

Basha   Sheige!

Maariya   Sheige yourself. And don't forget it's early in the morning.

Basha   Early in the morning what for?

Maariya   Early in the morning for you to shake out your empty piss-pot and put some solid ideas in it. Are we going to die paupers?

Basha   Die paupers? I hear you say 'die paupers' you early morning pestilence on a man's peace? Or my hearing dislocated by all the shooting and death screaming and grenade bursting from throwing out Rajinda's gover'ment? You telling me this pinnacle of achievement not deserve long repose of mind? Is this summer of our contentment not duly earned and richly deserved?

Maariya   Richly deserved, ha! You make me laugh. To be rich is to be rich, whether deserved or not is nobody's business.

Basha   On the rear-end of my favourite she-goat, I'll be damned if I know what dis she-cow she talking about.

Maariya   And don't talk to me about the rear-end of your goats. I know to what use you put them on those cold mountain nights, you goat-fucker from the winds of wilderness.

Basha   Be all that as it may – and I'll deal with you for that bit of dirtmongering all in good time – still Basha Bash not know what you are talking about.

Maariya   O-oh, God save me from this dithering apostate! He is so easily satisfied, I swear.

Basha   If I hearing you right, you say we going to die paupers. Now how that possible when this very moment we moving into all this new and sumptuous bordello, and with blood of former occupant making that special design on wallpaper, all mixed up with spatter of grey matter from his brains. Authentic grey mess, as myself can testify since is me exactly who put the silver bullet through his head. Now we have his mansion, I wearing his general's stars and stripes and long-service medallions on personal orders of my commander-in-chief, Field-Marshal Potipoo, and now you trying to tell me we still coming to die paupers?

Maariya   I said it, he is so easily satisfied! At least your predecessor in this mansion had brains – the fatty blobs on the wallpaper prove that. You, oh, I despair, when your head is blown open, there'll be nothing but soap, and not even the kind that foams. When I think of Rajinda and Moriya . . .

Basha   Moriya! Moriya! I think I telling you never I want to hear that name again. You two army wife can play at rivals all you want, I won't mix soldier business with woman business. You want to fight, go in her kitchen and slug it out with frying pans and soup ladles.

Maariya (*screaming*)   This is like a hovel to the palace they're living in, and you are satisfied with that!

Basha   They can live in the Taj Mahal or Buckingham Palace of London for all I care. Her husband booted out of office – very lucky getting out with his whole skin intact. I tell you I dream I flaying him alive and using his skin for cushion cover? Still, can't change that now. Potipoo for leaving him alone. But now this Basha Bash four-star general and enough troops under personal command to break into the Treasury. And if still now Rajinda happens to annoy me any way or try to make trouble, I get many way to make him know Basha Bash still around.

Maariya   And of what use is that to us?

Basha   Make me feel better for one thing. I still think he get off too easy.

Maariya   It still won't give you his palace. He's barricaded himself in there with his family, plus all the heavy loot from the oil royalties.

Basha   Moriya, husband and whole family can all go to hell. Wait till Basha start digging into that bottomless pot of crude with these very hands, right down to the elbow and up the stinking armpits, then you'll see action, you doubting me so much. You think all this time, I not studying how it's done?

Maariya   And suppose Potipoo doesn't give you the Ministry of Petroleum?

Basha   And what if sun not rising tomorrow? Just what the woman talking about? Take care of General Uzi, Potipoo say. He biggest obstacle to this coup. You make sure of a plughole through centre of forehead and you pick any ministry you want. Now is that plain enough for you, you doubting Tomasina, or I tell you what more Potipoo tell me?

Maariya (*flouncing off*)   I married a fool. (*Screams.*) Your General Potipoo is taking that Ministry of Petroleum himself, and you are the only one who doesn't know it. He's used you for the dirty job – as usual – and now he's going to pack you off to the Ministry of Goats and Cows.

Basha (*goes rigid for moments, mouth agape*)   Goats and cows?
What in hell the cow mean by that? (*Big grin.*) Oh, and me
nearly allow her making fool of me! (*Shouts after her.*) You
already congratulating yourself you had me fooled, not so?
There is nothing call Ministry of Goats and Cows in
cabinet.

Maariya (*re-enters. Faces him – withering contempt*)   Ministry
of A-gri-cul-ture! And that's also his way of reminding you
of your background – never mind your general's uniform
and long-service medals – and if you take one false step, it's
back to your mountain goats for you. Because he'll twist you
and break you and grind you between two rocks and spew
you back to the winds of wilderness whenceforth thou
camest.

Basha   You fooling yourself. My Commander-in-Chief,
General Potipoo, knows that I am loyal to the death of a
thousand cuts. Ask Potipoo name you one officer on whom
he place absolute trust and confidence and he name Basha
Bash.

Maariya   How many coup-pies have you had a finger in?
How many violent depositions and decapitations of heads of
government?

Basha   For that one, I lose count longest time.

Maariya   You can't lose what you never had – you never
could count – not even money, despite your abducting and
killing for its sake. That's why you're content with virtually
nothing. General Set-em-up and Knock-em-down! I've kept
count – nine coups-d'état to be exact. And I suppose all
those former Commander-in-Chiefs, Chairmen of Supreme
Council, Presidents-for-Life, et cetera, et cetera, whom you
kept knocking down like ninepins – they all had absolute
trust in your loyalty?

Basha   Of course they all trust me . . .

Maariya   And General Potipoo is so stupid, you think he hasn't learnt a thing or two from the fate of the others by now.

Basha (*petrified*)   You don't think . . . Shiege! Oh Shokoriko, protector of goats and goatherds! What I do to deserve this fate coming for me if this woman talking sense? Wait! Time Basha start doing some smart thinking. Maybe I keep discovering enemies to him – good job I keep Fatasimu – he real specialist at digging enemies out of wormholes. And when he see me eliminate them one after another, and with the ghastly tortures of first pulling out fingernails and sending him fingers and toes on birthdays of his children, of his wife, on wedding anniversary and celebrating each week in office, then he know that Basha remain loyal. For his first hundred days in office of course, I cutting off a hundred testicles . . .

Maariya   He's blabbering. That special blabbering when he's scared shitless, don't I just know it? (*Stops dead.*) Oh dear, I bet . . . (*Sniffs the air.*) I knew it. Turn around!

Basha (*backs away*)   I don't want to. Lef' me alone.

Maariya   You're disgusting! If you think I am going to keep washing your soiled pants for you any time you're scared . . .

Basha   I not doing anything.

Maariya   Go and clean up at once. I don't want any of your subordinates to see you as you really are.

Basha (*walking out backwards*)   Nothing here to clean up, but I wanting to visit toilet anyway. I have the runs. All other beings not like you who get stone for stomach. The rest of us human, have to run sometime or other. Something call obeying call of nature.

Maariya   Are you still here? Next time I'll really let the news leak out to the soldiers how their general leaks into his pants. You think I'm joking? Fatasimu! (**Basha** *scuttles off.*) If only I didn't need to preserve his authority! But things can't go on as they are, and if he doesn't come round to my plans, that's one threat I won't hesitate to use. All's fair in love and war – that's what they all say. Fair is foul and foul is fair . . . oh damn my pestered soul if I haven't caught the babble-babble of our son's tutor. My Sauna Bath has got it too – but then he's a parrot anyway. Doesn't have any meaning for him.

Fatasimu *enters from the house carrying a large framed photograph. It's the portrait of a general in full military regalia, dripping with ribbons and medals.*

Fatasimu   Did you call me madam?

Maariya   What?

Fatasimu   I thought I heard madam call my name.

Maariya   Oh, oh, I er . . . no, no, your er, your master thought he needed something. But he's gone to get it himself. What's that?

Fatasimu   Portrait of the former head of state. What shall I do with it, madam?

Maariya   Throw it on the rubbish heap. His time is past and he's lucky to have left with his skin in one piece. Throw it out and hang the picture of our new Commander-in-Chief, General Potipoo, a man, as my dear spouse General Basha was just saying, a man of vision and character and valour and compassion and what else, for whom my husband is ready to die the death of a thousand cuts. He said it this very morning. He says it every day.

As **Fatasimu** *turns to go, another soldier emerges with another picture.*

Maariya   Wait. What's that one? Bring it here. (*She snatches it, viciously.*) I thought so. Portrait of the First Family. Look at the face of that bitch. So where are you now, Madam First Lady with all the fine airs and condescension. Barracks bitch, forever on heat! Whore! (*Spits on it.*) Hang it up in the shooting gallery so I can do some target practice on it. (**Fatasimu** *goes into the house.*) I'll shoot out both eyes before breakfast, that should give me some appetite. (*Grins in anticipation.*) Afterwards I'll send it to the Madam Has-been as a present from the Second Lady of the Realm . . . Hm. Second Lady? Well, for now anyway . . . (*Exit.*)

Scene Two

Inaugural meeting of SCAR – the Supreme Council for Advance Redemption. **General Potipoo** *presiding. Representatives of the civilian 'legitimizing' bodies – the President of the Recognized and Organized Union of all Trades – in Mao suit and cap; President of the Divine Order of Prelates Ecumenical; and the President of Royal Estates Nominal and Traditional – both in full regalia. The Heads of Services are in full service uniform, encrusted with ribbons and medals – among them,* **Commander Bhieu***, Head of Rapid Disposal Corps, etc.* **Brigadier Tikim***, eyes bloodshot from a permanent state of semi-inebriation, nods off from time to time.* **General Basha Bash** *is seated next to* **Potipoo***.*

Potipoo   Now that the Divine Ruler has seen fit to place the reins of this nation in our hands, we must move to earn the trust of the people, and of God. The Supreme Council for Advance Redemption – note, by the way that the word Military is missing in that title for the first time in the history of coups d'état in this nation . . .

Council   Hear hear, hear hear!

Rout   Power to the people!

Tikim   Long live the people.

Basha   I say power to the people.

Shoki   We already heard that from Chairman of ROUT.

Potipoo   No, no, leave Basha alone. Our civilian members must see how even our top military are infected by the democratic virus. They will be our witnesses to the outside world.

Basha   Exactly what I am thinking, C-in-C.

Potipoo   Thank you. I welcome our new civilian members, all worthy representatives of civil society. Comrade Representative of the Recognized and Organized Union of all Trades, popularly known as ROUT, we shall profit from your ideological wisdom. (*'Applause' by the military members – this takes the form of rapping their swagger stick on the table or chair legs.*) President of DOPE, the Divine Order of Prelates Ecumenical, Your Eminence, your presence here assures us of divine guidance. (*Applause.*) Your Royal Highness the Chairman of the Royal Estates Nominal and Traditional, RENT, you bring with you the blessings of our glorious ancestors. (*Applause.*) Your combined presence reinforces our resolve that ours will be the very final military coup d'état in our nation. Democracy is the language of the world, and we have chosen to learn to speak it. We may stammer a little at the beginning, but with God's help, and the guidance of our civilian members, we shall become fluent in his new language. Our mission is nothing less than a revolution.

Council   Hear hear, hear hear. (*'Applause'.* **Dope** *and* **Rent** *incline their heads.*)

Rout (*gives the power salute*)   Long live the revolution.

Basha   I be simple soldier man, and only take orders but – long live the revolution!

Rout   Long live the Guatuna Army, vanguard of the revolution.

Potipoo   Thank you, Comrade Rout, thank you. And now to business. First item on our revolutionary agenda is: Eradicating Corruption! Now, if we must clean up corruption, we must begin from within our own ranks. We must take the lead. I propose therefore that all officers assigned to political and administrative duties must begin

with a public declaration of their assets. (*Deafening silence.*)
You do understand what I mean – bank accounts local and
foreign, business interests, property, stocks and shares etc.
etc. Any comments, gentlemen? Gentlemen! (*Some throat
clearing here and there. Finally,* **Tikim** *raises his hand.*) Ah yes?
Most appropriately, the Minister for Public Enlightenment
will offer us a lead.

Tikim (*voice slurred with drink*)   With all due respect,
Commander-in-Chief, I think that the gesture is well meant,
but might be easily misunderstood.

Potipoo   Misunderstood? Who by?

Tikim   It might be seen as a deliberate ploy for witch-
hunting. An atmosphere of witch-hunting is not good for
democracy.

Council   Hear hear, hear hear.

Shoki *raises his hand.*

Potipoo   Yes, Captain Shoki?

Shoki   I propose we begin with the public sector. The
banks especially. The banks are rotten. They are vaults of
corruption. Currency manipulation. Economic sabotage.
They mess around with our foreign reserves.

Council   Hear hear, hear hear.

Potipoo   I admit that's one way of looking at it . . .
Perhaps we should listen to the civilian point of view. What
say our royal fathers and the clergy? Your Eminence?

Dope   Er . . . hm . . . well er . . . Salaam ailekum. To
Allah alone belongs all wisdom. My recollection in these
matters, going by one of the scriptures which provide us
spiritual guidance . . . er . . . I think the advice would be – er
– Render unto Caesar what is Caesar's and unto God what
is God's. Ah yes, hm-hm, that would be the position of
Divine Order of Prelates Ecumenical in this matter.
Shalom. To the *orisa* belongs all wisdom.

Potipoo   Thank you, Eminence. And our royal fathers?

Rent   Well, yes indeed. Er . . . it's this way . . . our fathers have a saying which I think goes to the heart of the matter. If we don't eat yam on account of oil, we must eat oil on account of yam. Yes, that would be the advice of traditional wisdom in the matter.

A puzzled silence from which a handful quickly recover, with approving nods.

Potipoo   Indeed, indeed. Our royal fathers remain forever the fount of wisdom. And now for the position of our trade unions.

Rout   Revolution begins from the grass roots, never from the top.

Basha   Ah yes, never from the top. We need grass roots because we must grow from the grass, I mean from the roots, from the grass roots.

Potipoo   Well, we appear to have reached consensus very quickly. I am a great believer in consensus, so, let's move on to the main agenda. Agriculture is first on the list, I believe. General Basha, please report on your ministry.

Basha (*from a bulging briefcase, he heaves a pile of files on to the table*)   My ministry is committed to make the country return again to be feeding itself, instead of we spending scarce foreign exchange on importing common foodstuffs. The whole country will be mobilized to grow food. Eatable food that people must eat. My ministry therefore inaug . . . inaug . . . inaugrating campaign called Operation FILL THE STOMACH!

Council   Hear hear, hear hear! Brilliant. Kudos, Basha.

Rout   I guarantee the full organization and mobilization of all trade unions behind the effort.

Dope   We shall preach it from the minarets and preach it from the church steeples! An encyclical of unity of purpose will go out to all churches, mosques, shrines and cultic enclaves for a national day of prayers to back the effort of the government in bringing food to the people. A full stomach is more receptive to the message of the soul any day.

Rent   All obas, obis, emirs and other titled chiefs nominal and traditional will lead the way by turning half their palace grounds into farmland for cultivation of foodcrops. Feed the stomach and the people shall honour their ancestors.

Potipoo   So what are we in the army contributing to your effort, General?

Basha   Sir, all officers will be ordered to plant every available patch of land in their barracks. They must to produce bumper harvests within three months or they must to face court martial.

Potipoo (*excited*)   This is a moment to have lived for! A spirit of competitive collaboration between the military and civil society.

Bhieu   Permission to speak, C-in-C.

Potipoo   Commander Bhieu has the floor.

Bhieu   The Rapid Disposal Corps may be able to make a small contribution here, I am thinking sir. We offer the ministry our dissident disposal dump which has surely been fertilized by the rotten corpses of thousands of political dissidents and traitors.

Basha   Offer accepted. And thank you for mention of fertilizer because we coming to that subject in a moment. But to return to matter at hand – all the useless flower beds and lawns decorating the barracks will be bulldozed by tomorrow and we plant them with cassava and yam and so on.

Shoki   Oh, hold on now, take it easy Basha.

Basha　We uproot all polo grounds, plough and fertilize and turn them to corn field. We grow millet and vegetables. Lots of horse shit already scattered on polo field, and the turf broken by horses' hooves, so they bound to be all ready for planting.

Kpoki　Rein yourself in a little Basha. Just hold your horses, eh – in an appropriate manner of speaking.

Basha　But the golf course not having any horses stamping them up and down, it will need tons and tons of fertilizers. My ministry budget fifty million dollars for fertilizers to turn golf courses into juicy farmland.

Rout　Right on Comrade General, right on.

Basha　And not forgetting golf course is where officers plot coups, in between walking holes and making thousand-dollar bets per hole and drinking beer and brandy at end of match. I think I have some experience in this matter, not so?

Potipoo (*weak smile*)　Well, if Basha Bash himself says so.

Basha　Definitely General Basha say so. Officers' mess having too many ears and barracks full of walls with earholes, is in golf course the conspirators deciding which officer to stuff his head in lavatory bowl or bung through top floor window and which one needs grenade shoved up his rear end with pin removed . . .

Potipoo　Civilians present Basha, civilians present!

Basha　Sorry C-in-C, just manner of speaking so to speak.

Rout　Games like polo and golf are bourgeois affectations, decadent occupations of the leisure classes. The new democratic order, which must be egalitarian, can do without such reactionary pastimes.

Basha　Yes, yes, I am a common man myself. I rise through the ranks. Common rank and file soldier never play polo or golf except carry golf bag for superior officers. Is er . . . revolutionary idea? (*Again, with glance towards* **Rout**.)

Rout   Well said, General!

Potipoo   But Basha, I mean, the next thing you'll want us to plant cassava on our parade grounds.

Basha   Just coming to parade grounds, Commander-in-Chief, sir. Parade grounds also allocated to farmland.

Potipoo   But General Basha, the army must hold parade. No army can do without parades.

Basha   I already think of that, C-in-C. We use paved motor roads and highways where our boots make better noise and not raising up so much dust. We stop traffic and parade in streets. Make me feel good to think present parade grounds blooming with corn and millet and vegetables and tomatoes and goats and cows. Problem is – parade grounds also not fertile, just like golf course. So we need more fertilizers. Tons and shiploads and cargo planes full of fertilizers. Altogether, for first stage of Operation Fill the Stomach, my ministry calculate special budget allocation of seven-fifty million dollars foreign exchange. (*Pushes open file and pen towards* **Potipoo**.)

Rout   It's a rout! It's a revolution.

Potipoo   But the polo grounds . . . Now that we are democratizing, we may have a visit from the royal family. The Prince of Wales likes to play polo . . .

Basha (*tense whisper*)   Your pension matter, C-in-C. You leaving office for democracy, not so? You not beginning to think of pension or you going for retirement on chicken-feed army pension? Is fifty-fifty my General, you give me Swiss account number.

Potipoo   Well, actually, I bank in Saudi . . .

Basha   Done! I fertilize your account tomorrow.

Potipoo   Well, considering . . . (*Signing.*) Indeed, we must take the long-term view.

Kpoki (*whisper*)   But the hog is grabbing the entire budget.

Shoki   I'll handle this . . . General Potipoo sir!

Potipoo   Yes, Captain Shoki?

Shoki   With all due respect to General Basha, whom we all know to be a straightforward general, with unquestioned integrity, the mess that he has inherited from his predecessor may make proper accounting for such a huge sum impossible. Millions may again disappear into that bottomless hole without a trace.

The civilian trio begin consultations among themselves.

Tikim   (*leaps up. Declamatory*)   Democracy is about to be midwived by the military. It is an awesome, historical, and monumental undertaking. Guatu has the largest standing army in all of the continent. To convert hundreds of thousands of men and women and weapons trained solely for killing to the peaceful arts of agriculture, you think that comes cheaply? The Guatuna army is poised to set an example, to become a model for the continent for its new role as the backbone of Operation Fill the Stomach!

Shoki   The backbone? Yeah. All the meat is gone.

Kpoki   The military desperately needs an audit.

The civic consultations become more visibly agitated.

Shoki   An audit never hurt any organization.

Basha   Why now everybody talking audit? Anybody vote to audit General Uzi when he occupy position of Chief of Army Staff?

Kpoki   What a moron! (*Loudly.*) You've just taken over, Basha, so it's really General Uzi's tenure in office that we are auditing. Can't you see that?

Basha   But Uzi now dead.

Shoki (*wearily*)   Then call it a posthumous audit.

Basha   Postu . . . that meaning?

The civilian trio conclude their consultations.

Shoki   Oh, never mind. We're trying to tell you that it is not personal. Quite a different matter from er . . . declaration of personal assets.

Rout   As representative of the Recognized and Organized labour union, I support the necessity of an audit as the minimal condition of our continued cooperation.

Dope   We risk further loss in our dwindling congregations if it became known that we failed to support the principle of accountability. Give us something to take back, that's all we're asking. If we are to go out and campaign for Operation Fill the Stomach, we have to persuade the people that the military is also tightening up its belt.

Rent   Our very crowns are at risk. The army has made life difficult for traditional rulers. If we don't return to our subjects with something tangible . . . the people are angry, very angry . . .

Dope   We have put our civilian heads together. It seems to us the audit poses no danger to anyone. Except General Uzi, and he is dead, God forgive him his sins.

Enter **Fatasimu** *with a note which he hands to* **Basha**.

Rent   Amen. This is our chance to regain some reputation with our people. We're sorry but, our palaces may be burnt over our heads if they learn that we failed to support even this level of accountability.

Potipoo (*reluctantly pushing back the file*)   The military is split, while our civilian members are united. So, the majority appears to be in favour of . . .

Basha   Excuse me one moment, C-in-C. (*Hands over note.*) Seems urgent note come to interrupt my attention.

Potipoo (*signs of agitation*)   Gentlemen, it looks as if we must adjourn our meeting for now. The security situation has taken a turn for the worse. A bit of mutiny seems to be brewing. Some misguided elements are planning to take over Abaloo barracks in support of the ousted dictator, General Rajinda.

Basha   I warn you my C-in-C. Much better we have finished off that Rajinda longest time, chop his head in small pieces or nail it to the gates of Abaloo barracks for target practice.

Tikim   That's what comes of delaying a simple budgetary allocation. The soldiers' discontent is being manipulated by Rajinda.

Chief of Police   We had no report of this when I left the office this morning.

Kpoki   I bet it's all rumours.

Bhieu   We must dispense with rumours and dispose of rumour-mongers. I await instructions.

Dope   We see this as an attempt to derail the transition programme. The Almighty Allah, the God Almighty, Orisa-nla, Ogun Onire, Sango of the axe of thunder and all other deities and atavars, their holy prophets, messengers and angels shall take up arms against mutiny against constituted authority. I excommunicate them in advance and place all rebels under *fatwa, egun* and *epe* from this very moment.

Rout   In the name of the Recognized and Organized Union of all Trades, I formally denounce this attempt to derail the military transition programme to democracy. Long live the revolution!

Rent   It is most untraditional to rebel against constituted authority.

Kpoki   Who says there's a rebellion? From where did this intelligence report emanate?

Shoki   I bet this proves to be part of the ongoing campaign of disinformation . . .

Basha (*pulling back* **Potipoo**'s *chair as* **Potipoo** *rises*)   The Commander-in-Chief and Head of the Supreme Council has make decision of adjournment. We reconvene after lunch. Lunch shall be eaten in the Senior Officers' Mess, Special Dining Room.

Exit **Potipoo**, *with Heads of Services,* **Tikim**, **Kpoki**, **Shoki** *and* **Bhieu**. *The civilians follow.* **Basha** *is gathering up his papers, ready to follow when* **Fatasimu** *whispers in his ear. Delighted expression.*

Basha   Your Emnens! And Highness! And Comrade Rout – please come back, come back. It looks as if our dear wife has prepared special lunch to welcome you as personal guests of Chief of Army Staff. She thinking surely you deserve better than army cooking. Please, follow my orderly, he will take you to our guest dining room. Wish I coming with you but, this emergency . . . My C-in-C waiting for me.

Basha *sweeps his papers into a briefcase, hands it to his orderly and dashes after* **Potipoo** *and others. The civilians follow* **Fatasimu** *out in the opposite direction.*

Scene Three

An anteroom in the State House. **Maariya** *is pacing impatiently up and down.* **Basha** *storms in with a napkin still stuck under his chin, smudges of food on his face, fork and knife in hand, still masticating.*

Basha   What meaning of this? I just beginning serious closed-door meeting with Commander-in-Chief of my armed forces over serious security situation, then Fatasimu barging in again and telling me you must see me urgently. What happening on home front that become my concern?

Maariya   Yes, serious security business (*Snatches the cutlery from his hands and throws them away.*) Listen! We're ready.

Basha   Ready? Ready for what?

Maariya   There isn't much time. You have to act while
everyone is eating lunch. That means *now*! It was I who sent
you that intelligence report.

Basha   Intelligence report? What intelligence report?

Maariya   The report Fatasimu brought you. The so-
called mutiny and plan to attack Abaloo barracks. I forged it
. . . no, more accurately, I – doctored it a little. It was just
the routine situation report. If I don't eavesdrop on your
cabinet meetings and go through your papers, how would I
know the right moment to push you towards your destiny?
So I added the few words here and there to turn it into an
emergency.

Basha   You . . . you . . . you forge report? You send forge
report which I present as genuine matter to my boss the
Commander-in-Chief and Head of State? Oh Shokoriko my
protector! And when he find out the report not come from
Intelligence Headquarters but from domestic headquarters
of his Chief of Army Staff . . . oh I think he going to demote
me and deregulate me on the spot as first-class security risk.
Woman, why you want to get me into this military disgrace?
(*His hands go involuntarily to the seat of his pants.*)

Maariya   Don't! You defecate in your pants at this
critical time and I call even the common corporals to see
how their Chief of General Staff conducts his private
business.

Basha (*advancing*)   In that case I think maybe I just strangle
you with my own two hands, tear you to pieces right here in
the State House and prove my loyalty to Potipoo. Yes, one
way I sure can get myself back in Potipoo's favour.

Maariya (*retreating. She dodges him around the furniture*)   He's
gibbering again. How is killing me going to prove your
loyalty to Potipoo? Has fear finally finished off your mind?

Basha   I tell him you send me the note to get me to cause
rebellion and unrest and I strangle you myself. I carry your
dead body to cabinet meeting in my strong arms with tears

dripping down my face and drenching my ribbons and medals and I say to Potipoo, look, I love my wife but I love my Commander-in-Chief more. I kill this Jezebel for sake of you. What he say then? Oh yes he says, this man is loyal to the death of a thousand cuts. The Supreme Council break into standing ovation.

Maariya   Yes, the next Council meeting. There will be ovation, but not the way your retarded mind has figured it. Think straight for once, just this crucial once. I've had to think fast enough for both of us. When the Council resumes its meeting, guess who'll be presiding.

Basha   Who else? You perhaps?

Maariya   You're not far wrong but, it will be the next best thing – you!

Basha   What for? Potipoo not out of country or receiving dignitaries. He alive and well and I just leave him with excuse and now I must rush back to him. (*Going.*) Meantime, you say your last prayers because I telling him the truth of this forgery.

Maariya (*confronts him at the door*)   Potipoo will be taken ill. He will suffer from attack of sudden confinement. If you take your troops now, right now, to go and put down the rebellion at Abaloo . . .

Basha   Why you so much contradict yourself? You tell me just now there is no rebellion. You confess you invent the whole thing.

Maariya   As Chief of Army Staff you are in charge of troop movements. So? You – take – troops – your – elite – troops – to – put – down – the – REBELLION! And of course your other duty is to ensure the safety of your Commander-in-Chief, not so? So you replace the guards – whom you will accuse of being still loyal to that deposed bastard husband of Moriya, Rajinda, and thereby you – make – him – General Potipoo – a – virtual – prisoner.

Basha   You . . . you want me I . . .

Maariya   From virtual prisoner to prisoner for real. You find him a comfortable dungeon and then . . .

Basha   You asking . . . you . . . you . . . want I . . . oh this woman really determine to finish Basha Bash honourable career.

Maariya   No, just to give you an honourable career for once in your life. A career that others have been hogging, monopolizing, keeping away from you. Making you do all the dirty work. It's so simple. You've done it for others often enough. You did it for Rajinda. You did it for Potipoo. Now it's your turn and you don't even know which way to turn. Anyway, you can't turn back now. It's too late. You either carry out the plan or you're finished. All the service chiefs are gathered under one roof. Potipoo trusts you with his life. Rajinda is still stirring up trouble wherever he can. Now that is your cue: democracy is under siege and Potipoo is dragging his feet. Do your duty to the nation.

Basha   You're saying . . . you want me to take over power? I depose Potipoo you mean?

Maariya   Late, but the penny finally drops. The nation needs its redeemer. Is Potipoo a better man than you? Just because he went to Sandhurst and West Point while you came up through the ranks. But that's where you have the advantage. The troops know you. It's not so long since you were their sergeant-major. You are what is called a soldier's soldier.

Basha   Me, Commander-in-Chief? (*The idea begins to sink in, pleasantly.*)

Maariya   But a civilian Commander-in-Chief. Remember, this must be done in the name of democracy. We have to do some tinkering with your title.

Basha   Hm. Just now I agree to share the allocation for fertilizers with Potipoo. Fifty-fifty we make the deal. If this works, I can take back my fifty and keep the entire hundred.

Maariya   Chicken change. But still, it just shows you the kind of man Potipoo is. Corrupt like all others before him. Even worse. Taking fifty per cent of the budget from the poorest ministry of all, the Ministry of Goats and Cows. When he already has petroleum in his baggy pants. That kind of leader cannot be trusted.

Basha   Wicked sabotage of my Operation Fill the Stomach, thas what I begin to think. Keeping Ministry of Petroleum to himself and Ministry of Fee-nice.

Maariya   He needs to disappear into the winds of wilderness.

Basha   Hey. What I do about his loyalists?

Maariya   Like who?

Basha   Like those two crosseyed mongrels Kpoki and Shoki. All they do is snap at my heels whatever I say. Only your brother Tikim give steady support. He being university man, he recognize brilliant idea when Basha Bash talk. But I don't know which way Rapid Disposal Corps going to jump.

Maariya   As long as there is dirty work to do, their Commander Bhieu will back you. You tell them which way you want them to jump, and they'll jump. And then we've got Rout. Once you have the workers, you have the people.

Basha   Rout? Trade union man in this?

Maariya   All negotiations were concluded over the first course during our intimate lunch. The labour union leader will soon be eating his dessert out of your hand. (*Goes to the door and throws it open.*) Fatasimu.

Fatasimu (*off*)   Yes, madam.

Maariya   The General is ready to see Comrade Rout.

Fatasimu   He's waiting right here, madam.

Rout (*as he enters*)   General Basha, I've been informed that
I completely misunderstood your position over the Army
audit. Of course I should have realized that you were
merely carrying out orders.

Basha   Ah, yes, thank you, thank you.

Rout   We have to take something back to our people you
know, otherwise we can't justify our being part of the
Supreme Council for Advance Redemption. To be able to
tell them – look, the Army has agreed to submit to a general
audit, you know, after that, our people will embrace any
programme on offer.

Maariya   Tell him the truth Basha. This is no time for
misplaced loyalty. It was General Potipoo who was against
the general audit.

Basha   Oh, definitely, General Potipoo very much against
audit.

Rout   I knew it, I knew it. We all know Basha for his
probity.

Maariya   Thank you. Go and spread the word among the
workers. Don't forget the farmers and other peasants. And
the market women. Use Internet. Spread the word to all the
students. We need everybody to demonstrate in favour of
Army audit. Otherwise, Potipoo will overrule Basha and
eliminate all progressives on the Council.

Rout   Trust me, madam. The workers will set up
barricades immediately throughout the nation. There'll be
no compromise. It's – Audit or Sod it! – that's what we
workers say. Power to the people!

Basha   Auditor sordid?

Rout   Power to the people!

Maariya (*fishing out a large envelope*)   For the cause. We
know the Union of All Trades is seriously impoverished,

thanks to the anti-union policies of Rajinda, that wicked dictator.

Rout (*takes the envelope*)   Madam's thoughtfulness is deeply appreciated by the masses. This will enable us to start mobilization immediately. Our workers have been waiting only for this moment. When labour sneezes, watch even the Army catch cold. (*Exits.*)

Maariya   There goes the voice of the masses. Let's see what Shoki and Kpoki have to offer against that.

Basha   First thing now I bash them up and mash them up and smash them up, then flush them down the mess toilet.

Maariya   That's my Sauna Bath. Ice one moment, bubbling and steaming the next. Just keep the bubbling under control for now.

Basha   They think because they pass out of cadet school, they better than Basha Bash. I show them former goatherd know how to beat foolish goat into submission.

Maariya   Not immediately, you fool. You'll have plenty of time to deal with them afterwards. Let them know there is plenty to share, more than enough to go round. Follow my example. (*At the door.*) Fata, send in their Highness and High Eminence.

Basha (*nervous glance at wall clock*)   Hey, I think General Potipoo beginning to wonder what become of his Chief of Army Staff? How many more crowd you inviting to this party?

Maariya   Don't worry, I've sent some of my girls to keep Potipoo's mind occupied over lunch. He likes his bit of skirt and fun, you know.

Basha   When last I have Potipoo kind of skirt and fun, only Shokoriko my guardian deity can tell.

Maariya   You let me catch any of those army uniform chasers near you and I'll . . . anyway what am I getting

excited about? Who would want a face like yours which
looks as if it's gone under the treads of an armoured vehicle,
not to talk of the mountain-gut you carry in front of you.
(*Enter* **Dope** *and* **Rent**.) Well, at least the stomach did
inspire the entire idea of Operation Fill the Stomach . . .
(*The gentlemen knock and cough discreetly*.) Oh sorry to keep you
waiting your Worships, just talking of my husband's ministry
and his Operation Fill the Stomach.

Rent Your husband has our support, madam. He clearly
has the welfare of the people in mind.

Basha Oh, these two gentlemen are making very good
contribution in Council.

Maariya The family is most grateful. And as a small
token of the family appreciation . . . appreciation . . . and
expectations . . . (*Hands them each a bulging envelope*.)

Dope Oh, madam, you are much too generous.

Rent This is most unexpected. And unnecessary. We
were merely doing our duty by the people.

Maariya Yes, the people. We must now move the
campaign to the people – the Leader of the Labour Union is
already in the field. He is mobilizing workers and peasants
even as I speak.

Rent Then he can count on us.

Basha Auditor Sordid! No compromise.

Rent What, General?

Maariya The Comrade for Rout will explain. As other
three pillars of civil society in cabinet, the people will take
their cue from you. (*Takes out more envelopes. They make a gesture
of embarrassed refusal*.) Please, I hope you will agree that this is
no time for coyness. Times are hard but, the good shepherd
must feed his flock (*Hands over envelope to* **Dope**.) And the
ancestors must not be denied their libations and sacrifices.
(*Envelope to* **Rent**.) This way please.

Dope   You can continue to count on our support, General.

Rent   You're lucky to have such a dynamic wife General Basha. Her heart is with the suffering masses. The nation is most grateful.

Maariya   Thank you your Eminences. This way. (*Ushers them out. Through the same door,* **Tikim** *enters, followed by the* **Tutor**.) Well, TK?

Tikim   The search is over, sis. No need to look any further. (*Pointing at the retreating figures.*) You have just ushered out the image of the past, which now becomes the model for the future. Our ancient traditional systems hold the answers. We return to the days of indigenous monarchies.

Maariya   Our ideological guru has spoken.

Basha (*looks nervously round*)   Hey, how many people in on this thing? I know he your brother, but what that one doing here? He supposed to be simple tutor for our son and heir, not so? Why he mixing up in army affair?

Maariya   Will you please leave everything in our hands? All you need know is that the family think-tank appears to have found a solution.

Basha   What solution?

Maariya (*sighs*)   Oh, I've always said it's the father who needs a full-time tutor, not the son. Never mind. The orphan goatherd from Rukus mountains will now be prepared for his next metamorphosis.

Basha   Don't know what secret forces – metamo or whatever – you counting on, me I sticking to military and security forces to depose General . . . I mean to er . . . what I mean to say . . .

Maariya   He means to say, to impose general law and order on the mutineers.

Tutor (*heavy conspiratorial wink*)   Of course, of course, to impose law and order, madam. Perfectly understood.

Basha   Yes, I impose general law and order. And not taking orders from any outside forces.

Maariya   That's the spirit, my tiger. Always the reliable Sauna Bath. Just get to work, that's all. And don't worry about any metamo or any other forces. Maintain personal control of the military, that's your job. Potipoo finished lunch, TK?

Tikim   Taking his siesta – in er . . . very agreeable company. I told him to relax while I went looking for the Chief of Army Staff. He's expecting you, Basha

Basha (*exiting*)   Good. I oblige him. I take care of greedy generals taking fifty per cent of chicken budget from my Operation Fill the Stomach. He not careful now and go quietly, I think I fill his stomach with something else than general diet and give him general constipation . . . maybe I just give nearest crocodile stomach indigestion feeding on his carcass . . .

Maariya   Go after him, TK. You know how he is when his blood is up . . .

Tikim   I'll try and restrain him.

Maariya   Bloodless, Basha, bloodless, remember this still has to be in the spirit of democracy. Those western busybodies won't stand for any bloodshed . . .

Scene Four

Headquarters of the labour union. **Rout** *is on a soap-box haranguing crowd below. He is flanked by* **Rent** *and* **Dope**.

Rout   Rah-rah-rah-rah-rah . . .

Crowd   Rout!

Rout   Rah-rah-rah-rah-rah . . .

Crowd   Rout!

Rout   Rah-rah-rah-rah-rah . . .

Crowd   Rout!

Rout   I can't hear you. I said, Rah-rah-rah-rah-rah . . .

Crowd (*thunderous*)   ROU-OU-OU-OU-OUT!!!

Rout   How do you read it?

Crowd   It's Audit or Sod it!

Rout   Subtract it or add it.

Crowd   It's Audit or Sod it!

Rout   Let heavens record it.

Crowd   It's Audit or Sod it.

Rout   The state can afford it.

Crowd   It's Audit or Sod it!

Rout   Comrade citizens, your attention please. We, the three civilian members of the Supreme Council of Advance Redemption are agreed on this vital necessity for the transition of this nation towards democracy. We shall not budge. We have withdrawn the conditional support that we gave to the programme Operation Fill the Stomach until we have seen an open and thorough audit of the Army. I now give the floor to our lords temporal.

Applause. Shouts.

Rent   What do our forefathers say? If we do not know where we are headed, at least we do know where we are coming from? The Royal Estates support the effort of the Ministry of Agriculture, and call on our peoples to mobilize themselves in readiness for Operation Fill the Stomach. But – for the pouch of the stomach to stay replenished and healthy, the pouch of the Exchequer must have no holes in it. That is why we support the principle of Audit.

Loud applause.

Rout   And now for the words of our lords spiritual.

Dope   From the day we are born, a book of life is opened for each of us. No act, however trivial, goes unrecorded. On the final day of judgement, that book will be opened and each person, man, woman and child, shall account for his or her life on earth – so it is written down. And just as it is in heaven, so shall it be on earth. When the trumpets sound on that day of reckoning, only one refrain shall be heard. Dear Bretheren and Sisteren, let your voices be raised now, to herald the divine exhortation of that refrain: Audit or Sod it!

Crowd   Audit or Sod it!

Frantic applause.

Rout   Spread out through the land. Fan out far and wide. Spread the word, citizens and comrades, spread the good word.

Carrying **Rout** *out on their shoulders, the crowd rush off to shouts, unfurled banners, klaxons, mounting excitation.*

Scene Five

The Council Chamber. **Shoki**, **Chief of Police**, **Commander Bhieu** *of the Rapid Disposal Corps and some other members of the Heads of Service. Glances at the clock, watches are checked.*

Kpoki   I know the old man needs his siesta, but I thought we were supposed to be in the midst of an emergency. It's over six hours since we broke for lunch.

Shoki   I told you there was nothing to it.

Kpoki   Then what's still keeping General Basha?

Shoki   Milking the cow of opportunity, I bet.

Fatasimu *enters with* **Basha**'s *briefcase which he sets down at the head of table.* **Kpoki** *and* **Shoki** *exchange puzzled glances.*

Fatasimu   General Basha sends his apologies for being a little late. He's still holding consultations with General Potipoo. (*Slithers out. All look at him as he leaves.*)

Kpoki   Consultations over mere rumours!

Bhieu   We're ready to dispose of the rumour-mongers. I only await orders.

Re-enter **Basha**, *armed to the teeth, escorted by* **Fatasimu** *and heavily armed squad.*

Kpoki   Well, here's your chance to make a start.

Basha   Gentlemen, gentlemen, officers and gentlemen. The government escaping a very narrow escape.

Kpoki   From what?

Basha   From treachery and butchery, from stratagems and mayhems, from catastrophe and apostrophe. We would all have meet butchery in our beds or else butchery would have met us on the road. We were for the high jump, from Potipoo downwards. Fortunately, we have able to spirit away the Commander-in-Chief, General Potipoo, to safety for his own safety. In the meantime, he place us in full charge of all troops and troop movements in order to put down the insurrection.

Shoki (*scornfully*)   Do you mean we now take orders from you?

Instant reaction from **Basha**.

Kpoki (*hastily*)   Of course. As Chief of Army Staff, Basha must take charge until the situation is clarified. (*Warns* **Shoki** *with his eyes.*) What Shoki means is that we have to let the Army know it. The chiefs of divisions. And military governors too – I suppose?

Basha   Everybody. So let's wasting no more time. We use recording studio of State House – is through that door, all ready and technicians awaiting. You find the speech also waiting – your first assignment – time to broadcast to the nation.

Shoki   Broadcast to the nation? I thought this was a simple agitation confined to one barracks unit. (*Again,* **Kpoki** *warns* **Shoki** *with his eyes.*)

Basha   The nation is needing message of reassuring. News of an attempted mutiny is dangerous for our programme of transition to democracy. Minister for Public Enlightenment nearly ready with speech. (**Kpoki** *moves forward, heavily.* **Basha** *breaks into a big, affable grin.*) Wait till you see fine speech. Tikim read me some sentence – very full of democracy and how we fighting all danger to democracy and fighting corruption up and down and right and left and so on and so forth. Make the people very happy when they hear it – Brigadier.

Kpoki *stops, startled. Again* **Kpoki** *and* **Shoki** *exchange glances.*

Kpoki   Brigadier?

Basha   The sign of better things coming, my dear brother. And our brother here, Shoki, promoted full colonel. Tikim now brigadier-general. Everybody get rapid promotion before we become civilian. General Potipoo accept my recommendations. Is there. He sign it all before we escort him to safe hiding. So nobody can say is Basha promoting his friends and adding another star to his shoulder to make five-star general. But first we must dis'pline the mutineers?

Kpoki   Are there mutineers, Basha?

Basha (*throws his arms around* **Kpoki** *and* **Shoki**)   There always mutineers, my brothers. We are brothers-in-arms, so we must stick together. Those who disagree with authority are mutineers and only one answer to mutineer. Go on Brigadier, I think you will like the speech. It get signature of General Potipoo himself at bottom, so everything is, as saying goes, very legitimate. We have promise that there will be no more coups in the nation, and there is no coup, only a change of command.

Kpoki Ah, a change of command.

Basha So, just to avoid any misunderstanding, my humble self is the new Head of State and Commander-in-Chief of Armed Forces. And looking after Ministry of Petroleum. As Chief Officer Commanding, which I make you now, you will do the duty of broadcast to the nation to let our people know that everything is under control. Is right? I think? General Potipoo has peacefully resign, of his own free will. He is being assisted to pack his load and retire to his village where he planning to raise sheep and goats for Operation Fill the Stomach. No bloodshed anywhere. Fatasimu!

Fatasimu (*smart salute*)   Yessir!

Basha You now my Chief Security Officer. You give Brigadier Kpoki security to broadcast studio. See, I lend you my own security officer.

Officer (*rushing in*)   General Basha, sir.

Basha Yes yes yes, what problem?

Officer The Head of State – sorry, sir – the former Head of State has vanished.

Basha What do you mean, vanished? I confine him to his private office, guarded by the new palace guards. Who I place as officer in charge? Not you yourself?

Officer I never left my position sir. General Potipoo asked permission to use the toilet to make pu-pu. I granted permission sir. Some time later, I heard the toilet flush. Five minutes later, still no General Potipoo. I give it another five minutes, then I knock. No answer, sir. My suspicions aroused, I called out. Still no answer, so I break down the door. No General Potipoo. I searched the entire toilet room.

There was no other door and the window is simply too high from the ground.

Basha You dumbskull of a bonehead officer, you will face court-martial for this. You look everywhere? You search inside toilet bowl?

Officer I looked everywhere, sir.

Basha Find him. Track him down through the gutters open and closed, the sewer rat! Bhieu!

Bhieu Yes, sir.

Basha Muster pursuit squad and follow him through thick and bush. Take over the dog unit and follow the smell of his shit. You expert at that, I think. When you find him, do your duty.

Bhieu *salutes and exits.*

This is what we get for leniency and consideration – a fugitive on our hands when we already agree to be satisfy with just a prisoner. In fact, just place under house arrest. The military espriti de corps is gone. What a disgrace for a former Commander-in-Chief to turn himself into criminal wanted man.

Kpoki You're sure you still want me to make the broadcast.

Basha Brigadier Kpoki, you disappoint me, you really do.

Shoki The situation has changed slightly hasn't it, Basha? Potipoo is probably mobilizing loyalists within the Army as we speak. The elder son, Potiplum, is commander of the armoured brigade, while the younger, Potiplan, is commanding our peace-keeping forces in Somalia.

Basha The more reason to move fast, Brigadier. We must to take high ground initiative from him. We broadcast his resignation, only we add that he is now a wanted man,

wanted for spreading disaffection within military. You are
delaying, Brigadier Kpoki.

Kpoki   Me? No, I'm on my way. (*Quick exchange of glances
with* **Shoki**.) We'll see this to the end, I think. (*Exit, escorted by*
Fatasimu.)

Basha   A-ah, I always know you great nationalist and
patriot.

Shoki   And what are your plans for me?

Basha   A-ah, my brother Shoki. I am thinking very much
of what you mention during Council meeting, something
about banks, this may be a serious matter for economy . . .

Shoki   Oh. Oh, yes. The banking system needs to be
overhauled.

Basha   Good. Since you show interest in that matter I
make that your very first assignment. Summon a meeting of
all the chairmen and women and presidents, et cetera, et
cetera, of all the banks in the country. Bring them to the
State House for pep talk.

Shoki   Very well. I'll attend to it. (*Exits*.)

Basha (*to a plain-clothes* **Aide**)   Follow him everywhere. If
you see he trying to do anything funny, contact the Rapid
Disposal Unit. (*Exit* **Aide**.) But I think as long as he think I
give him banking cow to milk, he remaining loyal. Trouble
begin when he see that I intend to milk banking cow myself.
All national cow in fact. No room under this go'ment for
any sacred cow.

Police Chief   Any instructions, sir?

Basha   What! You still here? Why you not jump in
nearest jeep and join in the hunt for Potipoo! You wanting I
send you a memo or telegram or you not here when that
officer make report of escape. You not yet close up the
borders and throw roadblocks every half mile or what? I
wouldn't mind finding him myself so I can slice off his ears

and knot up his intestines, not to talk of claiming the reward myself. Potipoo did not treat me with respect – Minister of Agriculture! (*Enter* **Tikim**, *accompanied by* **Tutor**.) How now Tikim, that shameless fugitive surrender himself now?

Tikim   General Potipoo has taken to the mountains with nearly a hundred loyalists.

Basha   Well, let him stay in the mountains. We remain here in the plains and valleys which is where the State House, the Central Bank, Treasury, et cetera, et cetera, are located.

Tikim   Kpoki's nearly finished his broadcast to the nation.

Basha   Good. Now, what this new campaign idea you proposing to sell our new government to the world?

Tikim   You'll like this, Basha. It's good. It's sure to go down beautifully with the OAU. Tell him, Tutor.

Basha   Yes-yes-yes?

Tutor   Sir, we have come up with: Re-invent – the – Continent.

Basha   Re-invent . . . the . . . Continent? (*Savouring it for size and taste*.) Re-invent the continent. I like it very much. Yes, I like it. You think that up in your head?

Tutor   Between the minister and I, sir . . . myself er . . . have been done the honour of being coopted into the family think-tank.

Tikim   I sized him up when I saw him tutoring my precocious nephew. I said to myself, this young man will go far.

Basha   Good. I promote him Minister of Public Enlightenment straightaway. Because you must go to the OAU and the United Nations and you tell them, this is what we going to do – Re-invent the Continent.

Tikim   And we begin by re-inventing government. The whole world is saying – no more military rule. Good. We don't rule by the Army. But nobody can raise a voice against monarchies because they still have kings and queens even in European countries.

Basha   Oh, is good good good. I see where your mind going – we turn Guatu into kingdom, ruled by kings. Nobody complain any more.

Tikim   We hand over government to Council of Royal Estates, Nominal and Traditional.

Basha   Hand over to . . . ! That's crazy idea or what?

Tikim   Not if your humble self now became President of RENT. You still think that a crazy idea?

Basha   Oh Tikim, Tikim. (*He embraces him,* **Tikim** *barely endures it.*)

Re-enter **Kpoki**, *followed by* **Fatasimu**.

Ah, you finish broadcast?

Kpoki   It's done. It's gone on the national network – television and radio.

Tutor   Your Excellency, I think it is now time to show yourself to the people.

Basha   Where that take place? Can do it on national television, not so?

Tutor   A personal appearance would be more befitting to a man from the grass roots. Television has a way of placing a distance between the leader and his people.

Maariya *enters. She is dressed in extravagant traditional attire.* **Basha** *can hardly contain his uneasy stare.*

Maariya   I've just watched the broadcast. He did justice to your text, Tikim. History will record you, dear brother, as the true architect of the Basha dynasty. (**Tikim** *bows.*)

Basha   I tell Kpoki is very good speech. See? (*Pulling*
Tikim *aside.*) Must set to watching this master forger most
carefully, the way she forge Potipoo's signature so good even
Chief Justice not tell difference. She so good I think she
getting to forge Guatuna currency next, make herself richer
than even Basha in no time. I know she your sister Tikim,
but you not let her near Central Bank, you hear?

Tikim   Understood.

Maariya   Next item – to show yourself. The balcony has
been dressed in traditional motif. No more military images.
Locally woven cloths, carved calabashes, medicine charms
for fortification, beaded crowns and leather poufs, cowries,
iron gongs, chicken hoops, wooden xylophones, *kakaki*
trumpets, lion skins and elephant tusks. Twenty cows have
been tethered for simultaneous slaughter at the moment of
your appearance. You have to change your dress.

Fatasimu *gestures. Aides move forward with full traditional, but
Ubuesque attire.*

Basha (*unbuttoning uniform to commence change of attire. The aides
dress him*)   I know all about change of image and change of
dress for officials of new royal democratic government. But
why you dress yourself like a prize cow on show at
agricultural fair?

Maariya   You are simply uncouth. And ungrateful.

Basha   Is not fancy dress ball we're holding here you
know. This is serious business of change of government.

Maariya   The people must know their First Lady.

Basha   Who? What this First Lady agenda?

Maariya   The First Lady makes her appearance same
time as first appearance of First Citizen. The world expects
the Queen Consort to be beside the King.

Basha *looks round desperately for help. Everyone averts their gaze.*
Tikim *shrugs his shoulders and throws up his hands.*

Basha   Tutor, remind me how is going that saying I hear you talking. That thing about uneasy crown and so on and so forth.

Tutor   I think the General is trying to say, Uneasy lies the head that wears a crown.

Basha *sighs, moves towards balcony, followed by entourage.*

Basha   Very experienced king who first say that, someone like King Solomon who they say very wise man. Wise man my arse, when he get trap between thighs of Queen Sheba. Basha going to show himself wiser, so you wait we first take care of official business. Then I show you what happen to foolish cow when it prancing to market all dressed in ribbon and finery. It still going to end up hanging upside down in butcher's shop, though I think no butcher touching your meat except to make hamburger.

Maariya   TK, will you shut him up and get him to aspire to some dignity.

Tikim   The people await their redeemer, General.

They proceed towards the State House balcony. Already in place are the civilian 'legitimizers' – **Rout**, **Dope** *and* **Rent** *– plus* **Chief Justice of Guatu**. *Hostile shouts already emerging from the crowd.* **Fatasimu** *videotapes the crowd, whispers occasional instructions to his aides, pointing to a trouble spot below.*

Crowd
    Enough of army rascals.
    Down with Rajinda
    Down with Potipoo
    Away with Basha Bash.
    Down with the Army
    Long live Democracy.

Rout   Fellow citizens, we present . . . Basha the man of the moment. Basha the man of the masses. Basha the champion of the oppressed.

Crowd
> Hey, that's comrade Rout.
> Let's hear what he has to say.
> Why should we? He's sold out.
> Silence for Comrade Rout!
> No way. Out! Out! Out, Rout
> Out! Out! Out, Rout!

Rout Today, the people of Guatuna stand on the threshold of history . . .

Crowd And the Army again on the threshold of power. You're bringing in the military through the backdoor. (*Shouts of 'Out! Out! Out, Rout!' gain the upper hand over 'Give him a chance', 'Let's hear him out'.*)

Maariya Do something, somebody!

Tutor (*pushing **Rout** aside and taking up the microphone*) Let me at them. I have a PhD. in popular psychology.

Rout All right, see if you can do better. (*Storms off in a huff.*)

Tutor Friends, Guatunans, countrymen, lend me your ears. I come to querry Basha, not to praise him . . .

Crowd
> Oh, that's different.
> Querry the whole lot of them –
> And then bury them.

Tutor The evil that men do lives after them . . .

Crowd That's more like it. Expose all their evil!

Tutor The good is oft interred with their bones . . .

Crowd
> Another apologist! What good!
> The Army's no good – Get out!
> It's another military wolf in sheep's clothing . . .

Basha (*angrily, pushes **Tutor** aside. **Fatasimu** hands him a microphone*) These people all blind? You see me in military

uniform? Look at me. A man of the grass roots. I rise from
grass roots. No silver spoon you ever see sticking in this
mouth – all calabash for drinking and ten fingers for eating.
You ever see me play golf or polo like other officers? You
ever see me in nightclub dancing anything but own
traditional music? Never. Don't know even waltz or tango,
but try me out on makosa or high life or juju or suku-suku
and any rhythmics from any village.

Does a jig, spreading out his agbada *like a peacock's tail. A trumpet
blast from the* kakaki, *accompanied by drum rolls.* **Basha** *dances
ecstatically. The crowd applaud.*

Crowd
    Not bad, not bad. They aren't all bad, you know.
    I know him, he's Basha Bash.
    Never known a soldier to dance in public before.
    Oh yes, it sounds like a new tune, but it's still the old jig.
    Basha Bash is still Basha Bash, Chief Coup-maker.

Tikim (*desperately*)   Tell them Basha Bash is dead.

Basha   What you say? I standing here before you and you
tell me Basha Bash is dead.

Tikim   Figuratively speaking. Please, do as I say. Follow
up your advantage. Tell them Basha Bash is dead.

Basha (*grumbling*)   Don't make sense to me.

Maariya   Say it! I can see through your robes that all this
excitement has already worked havoc on your fancy pants.
If you don't do as I say, I expose your backside right now to
the crowd. Say it!

Basha   Basha Bash is dead!

Tikim   Speaking to you is the voice of the new
democracy.

Basha   Speaking to you is the voice of the new
democracy.

Tikim   I am merely regent of the new democratic order.

Basha   I am merely regent of the new democratic order.

Crowd
   Look, maybe it's not Basha.
   It's democracy in transitional robes.
   Shi-iaw! They're all impostors
   More delaying tactics.
   We're sick of musical chairs.
   Just who the hell are you?
   Don't play games with us – speak!
   Tell us who you really are.
   You're not speaking to fools you know.

Basha   Who am I? Me, I think I beginning not to know myself. I common man like grass roots. Like humble grass, I nothing. I own nothing. Former goatherd from Rukus village, but good goatherd, know how to look after goats. But also good Army record. Get nothing of my own to boast of. Look. (*Proceeds to turn out his pockets.*) See for yourself. Empty. Nothing. Baabu.

Crowd   This is just another trick of military ambition.

Tutor (*pushing forward once more, taking the microphone*)   He took the golf course, the polo fields, and he gave it back to the people for Operation Fill the Stomach. Was this ambition? Ambition should be made of sterner stuff. The Royal Estates Nominal and Traditional are here to back him. Yes, the evil that men do lives after them – but must we wait until the good is interred with their bones? King Basha is here to serve to the last drop of his blood.

Tikim   Not to forget – he supported the Audit of the military. I am proud to stand beside King Basha as the architect of a new nation.

Crowd   Has he declared his personal assets?

Basha (*turns out his empty pockets*)   I get nothing to declare. Look – empty. Nothing. *Baabu.* (*Takes off his cap and turns it inside out.*) Look. Not one penny. *Baabu kudi.*

Tutor (*whispers*)   Church mouse.

Basha   Whaddat?

Tutor   Poor as a church mouse.

Basha   True? Church mouse poor?

Tutor (*tersely*)   Yes, General, church mouse poor.

Basha   Church mouse poor!

Tutor   Impoverished.

Basha   Henh?

Tutor   Impoverished. Own nothing. Same thing – *baabu*!

Basha   Own nothing. Same thing – *baabu*.

Tutor   Indigent.

Basha   What?

Tutor   Ditto.

Basha   Ditto!

Tutor   God! Try – destitute.

Basha   What all this mean?

Tutor   Same thing – *baabu*!

Basha   Desiti . . . desiti . . . *baabu, baabu, baabu*!

Crowd   Baabu? Baabu? How will you provide jobs?

Basha   *Baabu*!

Crowd   We need schools.

Basha   *Baabu*!

Crowd   *Baabu. Baabu.* Go away. You politicians are all the same. We are tired of all your promises.

Baabu   But I promise nothing. Nothing. *Baabu*.

The crowd begins to throw missiles. **Fatasimu** *rushes him to a corner of the balcony while his aides ready their sub-machine guns.* **Maariya** *quickly steps forward, dodging missiles and fielding them off with trays and royal insignia.*

Maariya   Wait, wait, wait! (*Seizes microphone.*) You don't understand. The new leader has nothing left because he has given away all he has. To you, the people. Operation Fill the Stomach has already begun to yield full harvest. Look at those twenty fat cows tethered to the trees. They're all for you. Eat and drink till daybreak. There is food for everyone. The fires are being lit. There is *pito* and palm wine, *burukutu* and *kain-kain* for everyone to get drunk on. And you'll have three days on which to recover because he has declared a three-day national holiday. (*Positive crowd responses taking over. Loud cheering.*) Those huge vats over there are rice and beans and chicken and pork for everyone. That other side is for muslims – no pork will be served there. And vegetables for vegetarians on that side. No meat or fish. We have laid out enough eggs to beat the *Guinness Book of Records*. Yes, plenty for the stomach but also something for the pockets. The leader has nothing because he has sold all his assets and is distributing the money to all the citizens. (*To* **Tutor***, etc.*) All you time-wasters – you should always speak to the stomach – and the pocket! (*Signals to aides who pick up cardboard boxes.*) Here. Here it all is. This is what he owns in this world and he has sworn to take none of it to the other world. This is a leader who is truly *baabu*, but who is the most bountiful of living spirits. (*Empties boxes of notes over the heads of the crowd. A mad scramble for the cash.*)

Basha   You crazy woman! (*Stops. Grins.*) Ho. I suppose it's forged currency you emptying over people's heads for popular consumption, not real money eh?

Voice   If this is being *baabu*, then give us *baabu* every day! (*Crowd cheers.*)

Maariya   You are the one who should be certified for thinking such a thing. You think I would start circulating forged currency with my own hands, and in full public view. Those are mint-fresh banknotes I ordered in your name this morning. Why would I forge bank notes when I can forge your signature?

Baabu (*tearing his hair*)   I know longest time I must not only kill this woman but disembowel her with a rusty bayonet . . .

Maariya   First listen to the beautiful music coming from down there . . .

Crowd
If this is being *baabu* . . .
Baabu! Baabu! Father of the nation!

Basha   Hey. Stop! Stop! (*To his aide-de-camp.*) Is good Central Bank of Guatu money this woman throwing to rabble. Stop it. Go down and save some of it.

Crowd   He's the soul of generosity. Long live Basha the Bountiful.

Basha   Tikim, what name is that they giving me. I tell you I don't want no name like Bountiful!

Crowd burst into song: 'Baba ni baba nje'.

What song they singing now?

Tikim   They're singing 'A father has no equal'.

Crowd   Long live Papa Baabu! Long live Baabu the Bountiful.

Basha (*screaming*)   I not fathering anybody here. I not Papa Baabu and I not Baabu the Bountiful. Stop them Tikim . . .

Crowd   *Baa-bu! Baa-bu! Baa-bu! Baa-bu . . . !*

Tikim   The people have spoken. They have themselves resolved the dynastic problem we set ourselves. Long live King Baabu the Bountiful!

Crowd   Long live King Baabu!

Maariya (*turns to* **Dope**)   Well, what are you waiting for?

Dope   What, madam?

Maariya   The coronation, your flat-footed Eminence!
The coronation!

Dope   But I thought we agreed that would follow later. An
interdenominational service after this public acclamation, in
the public square, bringing all religions and believers
together.

Maariya   Don't you know a historic moment when you
see one? No wonder all your congregations diminish every
day – you're so worldly blind you can't see a Redeemer
even if he descends from the heavens in a fiery chariot.
Place the crown on his head.

Rent   What crown, madam? We were not invited to bring
one along, and crowns are not made just like that. A crown
must be ritually consecrated . . .

Maariya   We survive this day and see if I don't
deconsecrate your head on a chopping block. Improvise,
can't you? You notorious rent-a-crown kings – why didn't
you think of renting one? Make do with anything. (*Looks
wildly round. Seizes a conical brass fruit bowl from its tripod and
throws out the fruits over the balcony*.) Look out! Heavier stuff
coming down. (*Hands the bowl jointly to* **Rent** *and* **Dope**.) Use
this. Crown him while the ovation is loudest!

Together, **Rent** *and* **Dope** *raise the fruit bowl and solemnly crown*
Basha.

Crowd   Long live Pa Baabu. Long live Baabu the
Bountiful.

Baabu   Not bad. Not bad, I'm thinking now, to be
bountiful. Give me one box of spanking new Guatuna notes.
Time I do some spraying with my own hands, not letting
you take all the popular credit. Hold on there, my loyal
subjects, Papa Baabu himself going to show bountiful hand
to his children.

Maariya (*handing him a box*)   Hot and cold. Hot and cold. Life in a sauna bath would be more predictable than dealing with this feather-brained weather-vane!

Baabu   I heard that! Wish is you I throwing over balcony stead of this new-mint currency.

Maariya   Gratitude – that's one word you'll never learn. I saved the day for you and what do I get in turn?

Baabu   Is this you call saving my day when you not saving my money? (*Seizes notes and 'sprays' the ecstatic crowd below.*) Here is more. And more. And more. King Baabu the Bountiful say spend it all. Spend every last penny of spanking new Guatuna currency. Pa Baabu going to feed all his children today, so burst your throats as much you want with food and drink, but Papa Baabu going to make you all work for it later, you bet!

Act Two

Scene One

Baabu *holds court,* **Fatasimu** *in attendance. He enters to a fanfare of* kakaki *flutes, ceremonial drums and preceded by acrobats, tumblers and a frenetic talking drum. Takes his place under a traditional regal umbrella on the verandah.* **Tikim** *in attendance, in a smartly tailored attire. Two groups of civilians appear to be awaiting audience. One is a well-dressed group of bankers, the other a motley assortment – farmers, petty traders, unemployed, etc.*

Baabu   We King Baabu the First hereby declare first open court for common people of Guatu. We running open government, therefore every day we sitting here in open courtyard of palace, invite everyone with complaint or whatever to come before us and make open complaint. The motto of our government is – Open House – (*Quickly consults notes.*) – that being to say, Openness, Accountability and Probity. Seeing the King here, throne and everybody in open air, in manner of traditional rulers of continent, this already account for Openness. No more distance between ruler and people – is that distance making trouble and discontent and people demonstrating and not paying taxes and so on and so forth. That agenda of openness being finished, we enter Accountability. So now we look into accounts of nation of Guatu, where too much cheating and corruption going on in former times. All that going to stop now. Ex Brigadier-General, now Chief Tikim now bringing first complaint. Tikim . . .

Tikim   Your Majesty, the banking sector is refusing to cooperate.

Baabu   That not sounding good. That sound like economic sabotage – what you think?

Tikim   It's an attempt to starve the government of funds for the effective execution of its programmes, especially Operation Fill the Stomach.

Baabu   That still sounding to me like economic sabotage. We already pass decree against economic sabotage, not so? Where is Attorney-General?

Attorney-General   Right here, your Majesty.

Baabu   Only kind of general still allowed in government, not so? Now the world see we mean business this new democracy. Finish with generals one time.

Attorney-General   Your Majesty is absolutely correct. We are the only ones left – Postmaster-General, and Accountant-General and things like that.

Baabu   So what your department saying about economic sabotage? You prepare decree yet for royal signature?

Attorney-General   My staff worked all night to have it ready for your first open house. We think we have a decree ready for everything that may come up. (*Selects a folder and presents it to* **Baabu** *on a velvet cushion.*)

Baabu (*signs with a flourish*)   There. Now decree in place and already working from backwards, so nobody coming to say crime committed before decree . . . hey, you sure you make it function retiro . . .

Attorney-General   Retroactively – certainly your Majesty. It covers any contravention from the moment your government came to power.

Baabu   And before that time. It become effective from anytime we say.

Attorney-General   Exactly what I mean, your Majesty.

Baabu   Good. Now, what these banking tycoons coming to say for themselves? Those the well-fed, finely dressed fellows I see over there, skin smooth like that velvet cushion and standing as if they stuff all Guatuna money in their cheeks. We waiting to hear you, banking sector, this now open house, not like banks where you put all money in dark dungeon like common prisoner, not getting air, not helping fertilize Operation Fill the Stomach and so on.

Spokesman   With all respect your Majesty, the bankers' delegation has chosen my humble self as their spokesman.

Baabu   Yes? And which bank yours?

Spokesman   The Sankofo Heritage Bank of Guatu, your Majesty. I have the honour of being the managing director.

Baabu   Sankofo? What that? Never hear of any Sankofo before.

Spokesman   Used to be the Mortgage Bank of the South, but we renamed it in keeping with the royal directive to return to the past and – re-invent the continent.

Baabu   Ah, that is good. That is very patriotic. So why now you go and make trouble? You marry? I mean, you get wife?

Spokesman   Yes, your Majesty. I have a family.

Baabu   You give her chop money to spend every day, not so?

Spokesman   Er . . . yes, not on a daily basis, but I do supply the housekeeping wherewithal.

Baabu   Say, weekly or month by month or something like that?

Spokesman   Monthly, your Majesty.

Baabu   And she not give account how she spend money, et cetera, et cetera?

Spokesman   Well, not exactly your Majesty.

Baabu   What! You mean you managing director of important bank like Sankofo and you don't keep accounts in your own home? You not hear the word of wisdom which say charity begin at home?

Spokesman   No, I mean yes of course your Majesty. I am simply trying to explain that my wife and I have a system . . .

Baabu   Ahaa! So you get system. You head of family, so you get your own system. Baabu the King is head of family of Guatu, like I say before, he's like the papa of large family. So Papa send his representative to tell you you must follow Papa's system of accountability. Why you not cooperate with him, enh? Why you all give him so much trouble?

Spokesman   Your Majesty, we've tried to make him understand that . . .

Baabu   Understand what? You understand something special which Central Bank of Guatu not understand?

Spokesman   Ah, thank you King Baabu, the point is, Central Bank understands our position exactly.

Baabu   Then you already know that Central Bank fully following new system of accountability.

Spokesman   Of course your Majesty. As the main keeper of government funds . . .

Baabu   So why you finding it so difficult to do as Central Bank doing? You say you understand each other?

Spokesman   We are quite prepared to perform any function that the government wants us to perform. Once your Majesty's government starts keeping its funds with us . . .

Baabu   Look here you Sankofo man, seems to us you going round and round and this Majesty not liking that at all. You ready to perform function assign to you by government or not?

Spokesman   Of course your Majesty, that is what we're there for. Once the government became our customer . . .

Baabu   Government is everybody customer, not so? So, what you worry about? Now time for you to begin perform function which Pa Baabu assign you! Tikim . . .

Tikim   Your Majesty. (*Steps forward and places a pile of chequebooks on the table. Holds out a pen.*)

Baabu (*points*)   Sign!

Spokesman (*quick glance at the chequebook*)   B-b-b-but your Majesty . . .

Baabu   Whas matter? You not see chequebook before?

Spokesman   But this is the same cheque that ex-Brigadier-General, Chief Tikim has been trying to get us to sign.

Baabu Yes. Is own chequebook for your bank, not so? You saying you have no confidence in your own chequebook?

Spokesman   Your Majesty, this is still an open cheque.

Baabu   What your trouble? I think you hear me say from now on we all running open government? Everything must be done in the open, thas why we holding this enquiry in full view of public so no one complaining anybody making bad business behind back of public. You sign open cheque!

Spokesman (*beginning to sweat*)   Your Majesty, let me state here again and clearly that the banking sector is more than prepared to play its role in the programme for national recovery, especially your Majesty's pet project Operation Fill the Stomach. But we have to account to our shareholders and investors. We must know how much we're contributing here and there and then we know how to justify it to those who really own the bank.

Baabu   Too much grammar I am hearing this morning and is all taking place on empty stomach. Not very good for our Royal Majesty's tum, which beginning to rumble very bad.

Spokesman   King Baabu, I speak for all of us in this. None of us here has the power or authority to sign an open cheque.

Baabu   I see. Shove this fool into open pit.

Bhieu   With pleasure, King Baabu. (*Signals and a floor panel slides open to display a pit. He pushes* **Spokesman** *who disappears with a scream.*)

Baabu   And now Sankofo Heritage Bank fully belong to government. Soon as we can, we appoint next managing director. We take charge of bank on behalf of the people of Guatu.

Tikim   Next, Bank of the Middle East. (*Again, holds up pen.*)

Mid-East   Your Majesty, I think my predecessor has stated our difficulty accurately. What he did not have the time to mention – with, er, unfortunate results – is that all the bank managers here assembled, having weighed the importance of your Majesty's Operation Fill the Stomach, have voluntarily decided to make a contribution of . . . ten . . .

Banker (*whisper*)   No, make it twenty.

Another   No, twenty-five . . .

Another   Fifty. Get it over with. Fifty.

Mid-East   Fifty million dollars, your Majesty. Payable in hard currency. To be presented to your Majesty to use as you think fit.

Baabu   This gesture much appreciated. Now you sign cheque?

Tikim *extracts another chequebook, offers the pen. Relief on the faces of bankers as Mid-East banker prepares to sign.*

Baabu   No! Just signature at bottom if you don't mind. We fill in the rest later. Save you getting writer's cramp from too much office work.

Mid-East   But your Majesty, this still leaves it an open cheque. We are back to where we started.

Baabu   So you know that, you dung-matted tail of a bleating mountain-goat! So you know all this time you also wasting our royal time. I show you where you finish. (*Signals.* **Bhieu** *propels him into the pit.*) And the next one. (*The next in line is pushed in.*) Finish with all this business one time. And the next. And next. And next. And next. All banking now in hands of palace government. I think we take care of accountability, no? Tikim?

Tikim   No more government business for the day, Bros Baabu.

Baabu   Government winding up business for the day. Time now to stop this nuisance of rumbling stomach. You, go and tell our most unladylike Lady First Spouse and Consort to shake up kitchen double-quick time. Citizens, I invite you all to table with royal family. We lunch open balcony up here where everybody can watch. That way we promoting participation.

Petitioner (*steps out from second group*)   Pa Baabu! You haven't heard one single petition from the common people. We camped here since last night, waiting for this moment.

Baabu   You camp here? In open air?

Petitioner   Yes, Pa Baabu. With my family, wife and seven children, with one infant. We were thrown out of our house by a truly vicious landlord who tripled our rent just like that. Without notice.

Baabu   And where you living now?

Petitioner   In open air.

Baabu   See? Government policy already working. This now democracy, open society. You see my office here, also in the open. When everybody begin to work, eat, sleep and shit and fuck in the open, then we know we already reach the promised land.

Trumpets, kakaki *and drums as* **Baabu** *exits.*

Scene Two

Reception room of **Baabu**'s *palace. Waiting is a bunch of traditional medicine men, marabouts, assorted cult priests, crystal-ball gazers, oriental mystics, etc. Some moments as they eye one another covertly, with ill-disguised hostility. Some look into their pouches and examine amulets, talismans, etc. The Ifa priest intones silently, makes passes over his divination tray with his cowrie chain. An* **Oriental Mystic** *reads and mouths mantras; a* **Marabout** *tells his beads while another devout sprinkles incense from time to time.* **Baabu** *enters the adjoining chamber, followed by* **Tutor** *and* **Tikim**, *in his accustomed half-drunken state.*

Rent (*peeking through curtain*)   I believe his Majesty is now ready for us. Who was first? (*A mad scramble ensues.* **Rent** *lays into them right and left with his sceptre,* **Dope** *with his mitre.*) Back! Get back. Line up.

Dope   Down! Down! Where do you think you are? (*The* **Marabout** *slips* **Dope** *a bulky envelope, while the* **Oriental Mystic** *does the same to* **Rent**. *Both look at each other and reach an instant understanding.*) These two go first. Everyone else – Back!

Rent   Keep them in line while I usher in these two will you. Can you manage or shall I summon Fatasimu?

Dope   I've had lots of experience with rebellious congregations. Go ahead. (*To crowd.*) We're all brothers and sisters in the spirit, but that's no reason for us to get so carried away that we forget all mortal decorum. And *procedure*! Let me remind you all that we have a Ministry of Fee-nice, to which you have to pay some respect. There is the little matter of an audience fee, right? To the best of my knowledge, none of you has settled it. That's not nice, is it? I shall therefore settle myself at this little table and you can all come up nicely with your envelopes, which of course shall be used to determine in what order you arrived here, and thus, in what order you shall have audience with His Majesty, Pa Baabu.

Rent (*ushers* **Oriental Mystic** *and* **Marabout** *before* **Baabu**)   We thought we'd better bring them in two or three at a time Pa Baabu. Word of mouth is power of word, and since we put out the word, we've been beseiged by thousands of applicants.

Baabu *waves them to take their seats, which they proceed to do on the carpet.* **Tutor** *flips open a notebook and begins to take notes.*

Baabu   Welcome, welcome and welcome. Pa Baabu coming straight to point. The kingdom of Guatu facing threats from left and right. Too much dissenting and opposition and complaining and demonstration and so on and so forth spite of democracy and bountifulness which King Baabu bring to the nation. Uprising here and there. Too busy on this home front and not having time to begin to conquer all of continent. Operation Fill the Stomach hitting constipation. What future you see for this dynasty of Baabu? What we must to do to get rid of the danger? Too many enemies around wanting to topple crown.

Oriental   All the way from the continent of India have I come, with all the wisdom of the Orient since the days of the Kaballa, Kabuki and Katmandu. (**Tutor**'*s note-taking is noticably more frenzied.*) Of Karma and Kali, Kalakuta and Khalidasa. We have consulted the stars and plotted the alignment of the forces in favour and against this dynasty. The Wheel of Fate augurs well, augurs well, but certain things must be done. King Baabu must be resolute, for the star of Kali is in the ascendant.

Baabu   Kali? Who this Kali?

Oriental   One of the few divinities who truly rule sky and earth. She is all female. This means that the star of women is ruling the arc of disruption, perched on the apogee of cosmic crepuscule. You must beware woman.

Baabu   I see no woman. Unlike Potipoo, I always keep my nose clean. Only Maariya come even close, and strictly between you and me, she no longer woman – wait! Ho! Is she? Is Maariya maybe you thinking about?

Oriental   A woman close to the throne, not so?

Baabu   Where else she be if not near the throne! She so close she even get eavesdropping room for cabinet meetings until I smash it up. She forging royal signature all the time. She forge even her brother signature, he being member of royal cabinet.

Oriental   I knew it. *Cherchez la femme.*

Baabu   And she always talking how Gallup poll tell she more popular than our royal person. I know she cook the polls, but thas the kind of mind she get. Tikim, I think you promise me you make Maariya stop cooking the polls, not so?

Tikim   Bros Baabu your Majesty, if I'm not careful, she will cook even me.

Oriental   The throne is caught in the disruptive circle of Kali. The female forces of Kalakuta are permanently in menstrual cycle during the conjunction of sky and earth. Avoid female impurities. Be resolute.

Baabu   Oh yes, Baabu more than resolute. But how I deal with this woman? You hear even my brother-in-law, he too afraid of her. I think she get some secret forces I know nothing about. You know anything of er . . . metamo forces? (**Tikim** *and* **Tutor** *exchange reactions at the familiar plaint.*)

Oriental   Metamorphosis or metempsychosis – is all the same to Kali. Be resolute. It takes a woman to know a woman. You need to make pilgrimage to the shrine of Kali in my holy village and offer sacrifice to her shrine. I shall make all necessary arrangements.

Baabu   I think I come to see Kali soon. Very soon.

Tikim   We'll put it on the itinerary – either going to or returning from addressing the United Nations.

Marabout (*aggressively*)   On our part, your Majesty, we have looked into the Holy Book and it advises King Baabu not to make any journey. (**Rent** *coughs and sends him a warning glance.*) That is, not yet. Not immediately. Oh yes, I see a journey, a journey towards the Orient but, it comes somewhat later. First, Baabu must stay locked up in his bedroom, not see man or woman. Baabu must sit on the skin of a freshly sacrificed goat for forty days and forty nights. A spotless white he-goat. A new one will be sacrificed each day and Baabu must consume its testicles.

Baabu   Oh, that no problem.

Marabout   Good. Uncooked. Raw.

Baabu (*grimacing*)   Raw?

Marabout   Raw!

Baabu   Not possible I smoke it just a little? Add little salt and pepper.

Marabout   No spices. No condiments. No artificial or natural flavouring. Because no fires must be lit.

Baabu   Oh, thas all right then. Palace get electric stove.

Marabout   Electric stove shows fire. It glows red, evil red. Red is to be avoided. Even in dress. Baabu must wear just a loincloth of white. Red must be banished from the palace premises for forty days. Nobody whose eyeballs are red must come near the palace. (**Tikim** *reacts, then furtively slips on a pair of dark glasses.*) No red kola nuts, only white or yellow. No looking at red sunset. And certainly no cooker, not even a toaster. The fire inside them is the worst red of all. No true believer uses an electric toaster. It is the devil's own fire glowing from the pit of hell.

Tikim   I think I have the solution Bros Baabu. The microwave oven.

Marabout   Micro – what's that?

Tikim   No mention of it in the Koran, the Bible, or any other holy text.

Baabu (*big sigh of relief*)   Tikim, what I do without you, I not know. Good thing I marry into such intellectual family. You just save happiness of royal gut lining. Raw testicles? Urgh! Microwave oven do the trick.

Marabout (*amazed*)   Cooking without glow of fire? It is possible?

Rent   You'll be able to afford a microwave oven yourself when you get paid your honorarium.

Marabout   *Al-hamudi-lai!*

Baabu   All that settled then. First, I sit on goat mat for forty days, then I make pilgrimage to this Kali village to sacrifice to goddess.

Marabout   There is also sacrifice to be made here.

Baabu   I already agree to forty he-goats. What more you want?

Marabout   Your Majesty, do you want to render all possible opposition silent and impotent or not?

Baabu   What do you mean, do I want? Of course I want.

Marabout   Then you must foreswear all milk of human kindness.

Baabu   Milk? Last milk I drink is goat milk when I herding goats in Kalima mountains.

Tikim   He speaks in parables, brother. He means, this is a time for abandoning all delicate thoughts. For abandoning all scruples. Just what I've been advocating. Democracy is in danger. These rebels need to be smashed without any pity.

Tutor   Brave the poison of power, dare the doom of dominance, trample the terrain of terror, and be master of

megalomania – that is what he's trying to tell you, your
Majesty.

Baabu   Oh? Well, yes . . . our royal Majesty ready for all
that any time.

Marabout (*leans closer*)   Can I speak freely? Are the walls
secure?

Baabu   Yes, yes. I de-bug entire palace after I discover
Maariya operating private eavesdropping system
throughout palace.

Marabout   Then hear me King Baabu, and pay good
heed. Several years on the throne have been granted you.
Years upon years, if you obey the voices of your guardian
angels and grant their demands. Send out your foragers far
afield to find forty hunchbacks and forty albinos. The
albinos will be buried alive, with padlocks through their lips.
That guarantees that no voices shall be raised in protest at
anything you do.

Baabu   Must be albino? Why not use the rebels who
causing all the trouble? I like to see them buried alive,
maybe inside ant-hills.

Marabout   It is paper, the son of parchment that causes
trouble. And what is the colour of parchment, or paper?
White. Or off-white. Paper! (**Tutor** *stops taking notes, hesitates,
then hurriedly stuffs the paper in his pocket.*) But for that albino
paper, books would not exist. Newspapers are printed on
white paper. It is that albino skin that must be buried. It is
the albino lips, the talking paper that must be padlocked for
eternity.

Rent   What a bloodthirsty charlatan! Shall I throw him
out, Pa Baabu?

Tikim   Will you please let his Majesty do his own
thinking?

Tutor   Impeccable logic, your Majesty, even though
somewhat unconventional. In the field of behavioural

sciences, it does conform to the principles of sympathetic magic and symbolic potency.

Baabu   Enh? Oh, oh. Well, go on friend. What about hunchbacks? What for we need those?

Marabout   Our books tell us that in every hunchback are hidden the vital resources of life, far more potent than even the testicles. The hump, like the camel's hump, stores the power of water that sustains the camel over long distances in the arid desert. You, the King, are like that camel, about to embark on an uncharted journey through the burning desert. But the human hump is even richer. It hides the elixir of power. This is why the hunchbacks must be chained to walls and left to starve until only their skins and bones are left. Then the hump falls off, naturally. The fats, the moisture, all the gross elements of the hump would be ingested by the prisoner in his final days of starving, leaving only the secret elixir. We shall then reduce this core to ashes, and a spoonful of the powder will be stirred in your stew every day as long as you sit on that throne. King Baabu, I saw all this in a vision, as clearly as I see you here. Follow those prescriptions to the letter and your dynasty is guaranteed to survive for ever.

Baabu   For ever.

Marabout   Without a break. Overcoming all foes. Years and years of the bountifulness of Baabu's dynasty – until the crown is conjoined in the union of woman and beast.

General pause. Clearing of throats.

Baabu   What that mean, crown conjoin in union of woman and beast?

Marabout   I speak only from inspiration. I repeat the words from my vision. Until the crown is conjoined in the union of woman and beast.

Baabu   But what it mean? Rent, you make sense of that?

Rent   Yes, er . . . well now . . . er . . . I think I'd better
bring in expert opinion your Majesty. Excuse me one
moment while I consult my religious counterpart. (*Dashes out
and is soon consulting frantically with* **Dope**. *They decide to change
places.*)

Baabu   What the intellectual take on the matter, Tikim?

Tikim   Another parable like before, King Baabu. Or
figure of speech, more accurately. Like saying – until the
moon turns blue – things that never happen. He is telling
you this dynasty is guaranteed for ever.

Basha (*beaming broadly*)   That what you telling me? This
Baabu dynasty last for ever?

Marabout   Until the crown is conjoined in the union of
woman and beast.

Dope (*entering*)   The meaning is crystal clear. Until the lion
shall lay with the lamb. So it is predicted in all the holy
texts. It signifies a period of universal peace when all
creatures of God shall be as one under one command.

Basha (*nods approval, then change of mood*)   Got the whole
continent to conquer, so no thinking of peace until that
done. Then imposing of Baabu peace.

Tikim   *Pax Baabunia.* It has fallen to King Baabu to unify
the continent.

Dope (*crosses himself*)   *Pax Baboonia?* God help the continent.

Baabu   I like this matter of parables. Double the
Marabout's fee for today and put him on list of official
spiritual advisers.

Dope   Done, your Majesty.

Tikim   His Majesty is ready for the next candidates.

Dope (*announces as he exits*)   His Majesty is ready for next
candidates! (*To* **Rent**, *breathing heavily*.) No wonder you

wanted to change places. What was the other thing you were trying to tell me just now?

Rent   No time for full story now, but you and I better talk private, and soon. Situation is getting seriously out of hand. (*Catches sight of an albino and a hunchback among the candidates.*) Hey, you and you, I advise you to get out while you have your skins intact. You hear me, get out! (*Protesting noises from the duo.*) Here. (*He flings envelopes to them.*) Just take these and get out. Go! Go!

Dope   What's going on?

Rent   Maybe you'll hear it with your own ears. Maybe you even get to hear worse things.

Dope   Already I hear of *Pax Baboonia*.

Rent   What's that?

Dope   From what I remember of my Latin, it can only mean – Peace of the baboon. *Pax baboonia?* Human evolution is unravelling before our very eyes.

Scene Three

Battlefield. Two hilltops face each other. Milling around in the plains below are **King Baabu**'s *rag-tag army, hung about with charms, amulets, medicine gourds* (ado). *Some wear 'bullet-proof' traditional warrior outfits. It's a bizarre assemblage of outfits – from full combat camouflage and sprightly starched regulation uniforms to Rambo T-shirts, rap singer T-shirts, etc. Wedding dresses and G-strings worn over pyjama bottoms. The* **Tutor-Motivator**, *dressed in a three-piece suit with an animal skin over his shoulders, plus a headpiece with extravagant feathers, carrying a huge tome, threads his way among them muttering incantations and waving his fly-whisk over their heads, pours some potions down a few throats and flings trails of multi-coloured powder over them. The atmosphere is festive.* **King Baabu** *the First surveys the scene with satisfaction;* **Tikim** *close by;* **Shoki** *and* **Kpoki** *some distance away.*

Tutor (*intones. The soldiers chorus*)
    Double double toil and trouble
    Fire burn and cauldron bubble
    By the prickling of my thumb
    Something wicked comes this way

Baabu He's good. Tikim, must give you credit for good sense of judgement. That young man know how to mix old and new. Tradition and modern stuff – right mixture, very potent.

Tikim (*drunk and nervous. Starts at the slightest noise and the occasional sound of distant firing*) Yes, royal Baabu. But you know, I still think my good judgement would serve you much better in the United Nations, taking on our detractors and negotiating alliances.

Baabu No! Crisis time need all ministers around Majesty the King. You much too precious to send to the United Nations. Sooner I send this troublesome Kpoki. See? What I tell you? He already coming now with Shoki to worry me about something.

Kpoki Pa Baabu, with all due respect, where are the weapons my men are supposed to fight with?

Baabu Weapons? What weapons?

Kpoki Bazookas, grenade launchers, tank-busters, machine-guns . . . (*Reaching inside his pockets.*) I have the entire inventory here. They are all paid for and should have been delivered by now.

Baabu Let me see that. (*Snatches the list.*)

Shoki The supply transport was due since yesterday. We are exposed here with no means of defending our position.

Kpoki (*pointing*) And it says here . . .

Baabu (*screaming*) Don't tell me what it says. You not the only one who can read, I remind you. I know very well what it says and . . . (*Rips the paper to shreds.*) there, it not saying it any more. Satisfy? Now can I concentrate on my tactical plans?

Tikim   Yes, do let the King do his thinking. He's scored some major victories already without all this interference.

Baabu   Thank you, Tikim. I thinking your brother officers not fully appreciate cost of bazookas and rocket launchers. Before they even blow hole in enemy position, they first blow a hole in the royal purse.

Shoki   But Pa Baabu . . .

Basha   The enemy has no answer to our secret weapon. See over there? That man used to be my son's tutor. Did you know that he train overseas in er . . . in er . . . what that course again?

Tikim   Motivational psychology, King Baabu.

Baabu   Motivational and so on and so forth. When he finish with those soldiers they going be bulletproof and shell-proof and landmine proof and mustard-gas proof and napalm-proof and proof of anything enemy can fire in their direction, denotate above their heads or under their feet. (*Chuckles.*) At least they going to believe it.

Kpoki   King Baabu, what of the per capita war levy you imposed on the entire population, man, woman and child? Where's all the dedicated account from the oil revenue?

Baabu   Dedicated to the royal purse – don't waste my time with foolish questions. War is not market where you go and spend money. Ah, here comes intelligence report.

Fatasimu (*enters, video camera slung over his shoulder*)   Your Majesty, the enemy having infiltrated the surrounding forest are now advancing to attack from the west flank.

Baabu   What!

Fatasimu   If you look in that direction sire, you will see them just coming through the woods.

Baabu (*farts. Begins to quake*)   So soon?

Shoki   There goes the royal cannonade.

Kpoki   It's the missing rockets. I told you he'd swallowed them.

Basha   You here, Second Chief Officer Commanding, I think the last report say that they having four-course breakfast.

Shoki   And so they were, King Baabu. That report was handed to you over four hours ago, and since then we have been awaiting the arrival of the promised supplies.

Baabu   Upon my imperial sceptre, this is too much! First they infiltrate royal forest preserves, slaughter wild animals right and left, roast the defenceless creatures and breakfast on them fit to burst their disloyal stomachs, and then they not even have decency to digest breakfast properly before preparing to launch cowardly attack.

Kpoki   At this point King Baabu, an orderly retreat is advised.

Baabu   What! Fly in face of enemy? Never! I had high hopes, my COC, that no officer of the realm going to offer such cowardly advice.

Kpoki   My advice, if you recall sir, was that we should attack them while they were having breakfast.

Baabu   To which the royal okay was given, to best of our recollection.

Kpoki   And for which purpose the Army was standing by, awaiting the arrival of the promised assault weapons. You do not attack without the weapons of offence, King Baabu.

Baabu   Don't go on about the weapons, Kpoki. It reverberibate most boringly against our royal stomach and therefore we cannot stomach it. Hey! From which direction did you say they were advancing?

Fatasimu (*pointing*)   From the west, over there, sire.

Baabu   Then we shift our command post over there, to
the east, from where we can espy them more clearly.

Shoki   What are you thinking of, King Baabu?

Baabu (*growling*)   You remain here and you never find out.
(*Loudly.*) We shift the royal command post to the other hill
which royal strategy has sense to prepare for just this kind
eventuality. Tikim, are you coming?

Tikim   Certainly, Pa Baabu. (*Takes off ahead of him.*)

Kpoki   But the Army, what orders?

Baabu   Hold their position. Resist to the last man.
Fatasimu, take the same message to the Motivator, then join
us on the other hill.

Fatasimu   Will do, your Majesty. (*Exit.*)

Baabu   Where's Tikim?

Tikim (*off*)   Finding you the best route to the other side.

Baabu *hurries off in the direction of the voice.*

Kpoki   He sold it of course. Exchanged it for diamonds
with the rebels across the border.

Shoki   The pig is rotten.

Kpoki   I'm quitting the sty.

Shoki   I'm with you. Let's find Potipoo.

Kpoki   He might just decide to shoot us out of hand.

Shoki   Unless we go with a ransom.

Kpoki (*exchanges understanding looks with* **Shoki**)   Only one
thing can do that.

Baabu *appears from the opposite side of the other hill, climbing with
difficulty,* **Tikim** *assisting him. From the assembled army below, a
chant is raised.*

Crowd   Ree-Ree-Ree-Ree-Ree . . .

Tutor   Re-invent?

Army   The continent!

Tutor   Re-invent?

Army   The continent!

Tutor   Motivate?

Army   And renovate!

Tutor   Motivate?

Army   And renovate!

Tutor   Enemy bullet?

Army   Chicken pellet!

Tutor   Enemy bullet?

Army   Chicken pellet!

Tutor   Their gunpowder?

Army   Talcum powder!

Tutor   Their gunpowder?

Army   Talcum powder!

Tutor   Kaballah! Kali! Kalakuta! Khalidasa!

Army   Kaballah! Kali! Kalakuta! Khalidasa!

Tutor   Kabuki! Karma! Katakata! Kamikaze!

Army   Kabuki! Karma! Katakata! Kamikaze!

They break into a war jig, whipping up courage. **Baabu** *looks through his binoculars, grinning with satisfaction.*

Shoki   Look at him. Just look at the disgusting barrel of lard.

Kpoki (*going behind a tree with his gun*)   Still, it makes a good target.

Shoki   He's waving at us!

Kpoki   Wave back at him. Bow. Curtsey or whatever –
while I take aim.

A brief mime show of allegiance greetings between **Shoki** *and*
Baabu. *The gun goes off.* **Baabu** *is seen to fall, rolls down the far
side of hill.*

Shoki   Bravo! He's down, he's down!

Baabu's *army is startled by the shot. The handful with weapons
quickly seize their rusty guns, machetes and cudgels.*

Tutor   That must be our signal. Victoree-ee-ee-ee-ee-ee!

*Simultaneously the opposing army appears through the forest and are
checked in stride by the weirdly costumed assortment of soldiers,
including a fully armoured figure. The* **Tutor-Motivator** *is in
their midst, waving his fly-whisk round and round over their heads.*

Aroint thee witch, aroint thee!

Army   Aroint thee, witch, aroint thee!

Tutor   Out, out, damned spot!

Army   Out, out, damned spot!

Tutor   By the prickling of my thumb something wicked
comes this way.

Army   By the prickling of my thumb, something wicked
comes this way.

Leader   It's Baabu's rabble. Follow me, they're finished!
(*He charges forward.*)

Soldier   What rabble? They're witches. Sorcerers. No
bullets can touch them.

*Throws down his weapon and flees. Others panic and follow suit.
General rout.* **Leader** *has charged forward, turns round and finds
himself isolated.*

Leader   What the . . . !

A shot rings out from **Baabu***'s ranks.* **Leader** *falls.* **Baabu***, who had fallen on the far side of the hill, now staggers in from behind the hill, stumbles and rolls, landing on the* **Leader***'s corpse. The sight of* **Baabu***, covered in mud and dried twigs, and holding a corkscrewed crown before him like a talisman, also puts his own soldiers to flight in the opposite direction, leaving him alone in the field.*

Baabu   Oh my suffering ancestors, what a to-do! Really. Must do something about our royal corpus before it turns corpse. And just see what that tumble done to royal crown. (*Tries to straighten it.*) All squashed and twisted and crooked. Have to commission another, more befitting royal status, this time make it twenty-carat gold and shining full of diamonds and likewise jewels. (*Looks around, finds he's alone on the field of battle.*) Seems we have been here before, alone and dominating field of victory as far as eye can see. Seems Baabu way of life, I beginning to think. (*Sees the corpse and quickly extricates himself.*) What! And what's this then? Well, if I haven't gone and killed . . . Well well, it is the leader of rebel band himself. So, my friend, where now all your revolutionary clatter, you Chairman Mao and Marx Brothers and Fidel Castro all roll in one? Blow my favourite goat if I haven't gone and massacred you in the greatest hand-to-hand combat in history of warfare, all by myself! Oh, I'd better just make sure. (*Feels around for his dagger.*) Where is my trusty poison-tip poignard so I can apply the coup de grâce? (*His hands reach his stomach and he pauses.*) Oh my God, if that roundpoint of the anatomy has not been torn to pieces! All that ripping and disembowelling happen when I rolling down the hill or . . . my God! I've been shot! Shit! Some mad rebel take potshot at royal tum and damn if he hasn't blown a hole right through me. (*Thrusts his fist into his stomach. It is stopped. A big grin comes over his face.*) Ha ha! No wonder they say is wise king always carry his ransom on his body. Where would we be without this expensive body armour, enh? Next time that Minister of Fee-nice tell me I not carry the Central Bank on my body, I put him in iron safe and throw him in shitpit. It's these thick wads of mint-fresh notes save our royal intestines. (*Starts pulling out the* *bundles. Turns maudlin.*) But what a mess! The royal nest-egg all torn to shreds, that's for sure. I don't know if that such good bargain after all. Oh you, don't think I've forgotten you. (*Begins to wrestle the lifeless corpse in a series of dramatic 'wrestling' holds, including a flying leap on it, paunch first. Finally begins to stab it repeatedly.*) Take that! And that! And that! That's for causing the royal Treasury the grief of being torn to pieces and rendered worthless on the money market, you poltroon, you anarchist pauper, you bearded convolutionary!

Begins sorting out his money, laying some notes aside and discarding others. **Shoki** *and* **Kpoki**, *searching the slopes for* **Baabu**'s *body, reappear.*

Shoki   I know you hit him fair and square. I could hear the dum-dum bullet strike and tear into his rotted guts.

Kpoki   He fell, that much I'm certain of. But where's Tikim? I hope he hasn't made off with the body.

Shoki   No. He'd have fled the moment he saw his master fall.

Kpoki (*looks up, eyes widening in disbelief*)   Shoki . . .

Shoki   What?

Kpoki   Look over there!

Shoki   What is it? My God!

Kpoki   No, our Devil.

Shoki   Am I hallucinating?

Kpoki   No. He's real enough. What's he up to?

Shoki (*reaching for his pistol*)   He's all alone. This time . . .

Kpoki   We'd better first make sure. Fatasimu . . . even Tikim may be lurking nearby.

Shoki   We'll soon find out. Is that you, your Most Royal Highness?

Kpoki   How fare you, dear King Baabu?

Startled, **Baabu** *starts to stuff the notes back in his belly-pouch, scrambles to his feet. Gives the rebel* **Leader***'s corpse several kicks.*

Baabu   I knock him out. He real tough one but I take him out single-handed – give me the hand-to-hand fighting any day and Basha Bash make himself at home. I put the rest of his rebel band to rout of course. He should have followed their example but oh no, he think to challenge me to single combat . . . talking of which . . . (*Looks around.*) Where is our royal land force?

Kpoki *and* **Shoki** *quickly exchange glances.*

Kpoki   Evaporated, I would say. We met them on the other side of the hill, running like mad. But what the hell was chasing them? We saw no enemy forces.

Baabu   They giving chase to the scattered rebels and carrying out mopping-up operations, no doubt. We fight battle of strategy, Brigadier Kpoki. Time to advance, time to retreat, time to wallop enemy, time to give chase when they scatter.

Shoki   But they've exposed your Majesty to danger.

Kpoki   I mean, your Majesty has been left all alone . . .

As they advance on him, **Tikim** *enters backwards, as if expecting attack from every direction, bloodied machete in hand and two severed heads slung across a shoulder.* **Kpoki** *and* **Shoki** *exchange looks of disbelief.*

Baabu   Aha! (**Tikim** *nearly jumps out of his skin.*) Here comes our vanishing brother-in-law and Minister of Foreign Affairs. How now Tikim? Fine time you pick to go awol, we're thinking. Oh! You been chasing head trophy now I see?

Tikim   Awol, your Royal Majesty, awol? You do me grave injustice, sire. I have been in pursuit of the enemy and separating their heads from their shoulders. Tough necks these rebels have. I think I have sprained my shoulder.

Shoki (*contemptuously*)   Whose corpses did you rob of those trophies, Tikim?

Kpoki   Since when did you start wielding a machete?

Baabu (*casts a triumphant look at the two*)   I told you. Battle is all matter of strategy. Moment to evacuate, moment to eviscerate and decapitate.

Shoki   Did you really decapitate the enemy, Tikim? Live, that is!

Tikim   You're simply eaten up with jealousy. And inferiority complex. Because I am a university graduate, you think that makes me less of a soldier? You need brains even in war, let me remind you.

Baabu   What? Of course you need brains to fight war. But where are the rest of the loyal troops, Tikim?

Tikim   I came to lead you to them. We came upon the rebel camp in flight – I mean, in the course of pursuing the enemy in their flight. So now we've taken it over and secured the camp which, you will be pleased to hear, is not only fully equipped with weapons of offensive and defensive and mass destruction, but is actually still pungent with the aroma of roasting warthogs, giraffes and antelopes barely consumed, an elephant on an improvised spit between two trees (**Baabu** *begins to drool.*), assorted rodents, rhesus monkeys, crocodiles and alligators *en casserole*, at least two standing giraffes with their legs implanted in hard baked clay ovens and heads nailed to trees while the fire of slow roast tickles their excavated interior . . .

Baabu   Lead on Tikim, guide our royal feet to the feast . . .

Tikim   I have not mentioned, your Majesty, that we have seized their cache of elephant tusks, and rhinoceros horns . . .

Baabu   Ivory! Ivory is gold! But his brother, the
rhinoceros horn . . . Tikim, you know what rhinoceros horn
do?

Tikim   The rhino charges with it, I know.

Baabu   How come you so ignorant with all book you
read. You not know when rhinoceros horn is ground to
powder it . . . it . . . it er . . . oh, you know, Tikim . . . I
mean, longest time this royal tum allow Majesty to see if
natural sceptre still there or not. Not even sure if still
kicking, seeing as no encouragement or provocation coming
from royal spouse these many years, I've lost count. Your
sister turn me into monk, Tikim.

Tikim   Oh, if that's all, leave that to me. We have no
shortage of camp followers.

Baabu   Might be good to have rhinoceros power around
when that happen.

Tikim   Come on, you are the picture of virility. But, all
right. Leave it to me.

Fatasimu (*enters*)   The enemy has been put to rout, your
Majesty. Her Excellency the First Lady sends her greetings
on this immense victory, news of which reached her in the
midst of launching her latest charitable project.

Baabu   Another project? What's that?

Fatasimu   Better Life for Frugal Women.

Baabu   Expensive shit! Still it keeps her busy not
interfering with royal matters.

Fatasimu   She cannot wait to express her sentiments of
admiration in her own person.

Baabu   Too bad. She get to wait, like everybody.

Fatasimu   Her Ladyship is already there at the camp,
awaiting your arrival.

Baabu   At the camp already? Who let her in? You not posting guards? She finish the food before we arrive. Come on, Tikim, we better hurry. And remind me to deal with whoever letting that voracious virago into the camp before our royalty.

Tikim   My sister is a difficult woman to stop.

Fatasimu   And she did arrive in company of your beloved son and heir.

Baabu   Worse and worse. He even more greedy than his mother. Come on, come on, stop talking and making excuses. Lead us to the camp.

Exit, with **Tikim** *and* **Fatasimu**. **Fatasimu** *dodges behind a tree, whips out a snooper microphone which he extends as he eavesdrops on the other two.*

Shoki   Think we'll ever get another chance?

Kpoki   No, let's take our chance with Potipoo.

Scene Four

Nightfall. The captured rebel camp. **Baabu** *and* **Maariya** *are sprawled over boulders, and tree trunks hewn into benches and eating surfaces. Huge cadavers of partly consumed game, bones, strips of skin and meat are scattered all over the camp. Outsize wine gourds and drinking calabashes. Crude stills are bubbling, soldiers stagger in to help themselves to fermented liquor. Weapons litter the ground, dangle from tree branches and prop up wooden trays of food.* **Tikim** *is snoring, drunk and bloated.* **Maariya**'s *face and dress are smeared in meat juices. She looks every bit as sated as her spouse but keeps an alert eye on surroundings, reacting at any sudden or unusual sound.*

Baabu (*drowsily*)   Re-invent . . .

Maariya   Shee-it!

Baabu   . . . the continent. (*He burps.*)

Maariya   Takes one incontinent to know another.

Baabu   Sheige to you too! You looking specially foul this afternoon. In new continent I must to pass royal decree against women looking foul and ugly like you.

Maariya   Must be a long time since you looked in the mirror.

Baabu (*looks around*)   Those rebels certainly know how to live good life.

Maariya   Ye-eah. Listen Basha Boy, now that your rag-tag army has tasted this Robin Hood life, you think they'll want to go back to the mangy leftovers from your right royal table?

Baabu   Watch your mouth Lady King, that kind of talk coming close to treason, spreading of alarm and discontent and, consequently, incitement. Be careful we don't put you on traditional trial, tie you to tree of repentance and be pelted by rotten venison and fermenting liquor by the rabble, you being such rabble-rouser. Is king's right in traditional custom, I hope you remember.

Maariya   Shee-it! Try it and you'll learn whose popularity ratings are higher. You'll be shamed to see the First Consort garlanded in flowers and sprayed in the fragrance of Cartier's *Nuits du Continent* . . .

Baabu   Ho. Next she'll be wanting to have bath in asses' milk.

Maariya   Why not? Moriya had a bubble bath every day didn't she?

Baabu   So what?

Maariya   So what? The bubbles came from champagne you nitpocket. And no simple Moët et Chandon for her ladyship, oh no. It had to be Pol Roger or Lanson, and nothing but pink if you please. She wanted Kristal, but the

French embassy put its foot down when they found out to what use she was putting the bubbly.

Baabu   Don't know all brandname you calling, but she never smell any better for them. And you smell worse. You smell like something remind me of cat shit, tell you truth . . .

Maariya   Fill your mouth with all the shit you want, just don't let it come out of your pants again, I'm warning you! I can tell on you any time, I swear.

Baabu   Oh, shut up. We need some royal distraction. Fatasimu!

Fatasimu (*entering*)   Your Majesty?

Baabu   Send in our heir apparent and prepare to serve trussed chicken.

Exit **Fatasimu**.

Maariya   I suppose now you want him to be trained to become as big a glutton as you. Look, just look at this. Your commanders are in the field of action, when they return they'll find only skin and bones. And you have consumed all the palm wine.

Baabu   Why they not seize their own booty and loot and rape to their bloody heart's content? Has royal proclamation not provide them forty-eight-hour liberty rampage through every conquered city, village and hamlet? We not giving them liberty to ravage and pillage and mutilate and copulate to their hearts' content?

Enter **Tutor-Motivator**, *with son*, **Biibabae**, *in tow*.

Tutor   Your Majesty!

Baabu   Our son! Come, heir apparent, come into the embrace of your all-victorious father.

Biibabae *stands and looks around the scene of devastation. Puckered nose.*

Biibabae   Was this all your doing?

Baabu (*sheepishly*)   I had a little help, naturally. Not wanting you to think your father that greedy. Your mother play her own part, if you must know.

Maariya   Keep me out of it.

Baabu   Come, son and heir give your father a victory hug.

Biibabae   My tutor says it was an unprecedented victory.

Maariya   Give your father a hug and be done with it. There's already too much song and dance about a minor skirmish – don't you go and add to his royal flatulence.

Biibabae (*shrugs. Approaches and stops dead.*)   Oh. You stink.

Baabu   Silly boy. You think trenches are your hairdressing salons. When you sleep rough with your troops, mucking up with them in swamps and dunghills and horse stables and what else to prove royal leadership . . . of course I stink. That is noble stench of a warrior, manly and royal. Embrace it, son and heir.

Biibabae   Not until you've had a bath. The other soldiers don't stink half as much as you do.

Baabu   Well, a king must set example for his subjects to follow . . .

Biibabae   And you still haven't turned over the diamond mines you promised for my seventh birthday. That stinks even worse. Now I even have to eat your leftovers. (*Settles down to feasting.*)

Baabu (*delighted. To* **Tutor**)   He real genius. I know he born genius. No need to consult soothsayer to tell me he growing up to be just like his father.

Maariya   One Sauna Bath in the family – and one who never takes a bath – is already one too many.

Baabu   Ignore her. She get that way after eating giraffe udders and over two dozen sun-dried crocodile nipples. So now she thinks she crocodile. Wish she were. At least her hide become useful for something. Come on Tutor-Motivator, how goes the upbringing and training? How he react to lower classes and all that riff-raff? He take to cracking the whip on whimpering peasants?

Tutor   With charming enthusiasm, your Majesty.

Baabu   What hobbies he like now? That way we can tell if he get rounded development like his father.

Maariya (*looking at his stomach*)   God forbid!

Fatasimu (*entering*)   One trussed chicken coming up, your Majesty.

He pushes in a captive rebel, trunk encased in what looks like a chicken coop, his head poking out from the top.

Maariya (*penny drops, bursts into raucous laughter*)   Why, you dung-matted fur on the rear end of a mountain goat, if you didn't have me well and truly fooled this time! And me thinking trussed chicken was just another item on the banquet.

Baabu (*shyly, gratified*)   Oh, well, so you like it then?

Maariya   Like it? You devious cook, of all the chickens I've ever served – roasted, basted, fricasseed, stuffed, grilled and pickled, did you ever see the like of it? Which of them is it?

Fatasimu   The rebel spy we caught trying to infiltrate the camp, your Excellency.

Baabu   Fatasimu smell him out like dog shit.

Fatasimu *forcibly positions him so his legs straddle a still smouldering fire.* **Maariya** *claps with delight.*

Maariya   That should stop him catching a cold.

Fatasimu   Indeed, madam.

Baabu   You tenderize him? Served him the *fatasimu* garnish?

Fatasimu   I try to live up to my name, your Excellency. When the pepper shot up his nostrils, he nearly suffered terminal convulsions.

Baabu   Nothing can make a rebel palatable, mind you. A rebel is the stringiest mammal of God's creation, totally indigestible and inimical to state and stomach.

Fatasimu   We arranged a special toy for the royal prince.

Baabu   Oh, our heir apparent. I'd forgotten all about him.

Biibabae (*discarding a chunk of meat*)   You always forget all about me. When you've all finished having your fun, that's when you remember I exist.

Baabu   Don't be petulant now. It not become your blue blood. Anyway, we did not wish interrupt your breakfast, or brunch. You ready for your manhood test?

Fatasimu   Fortunately the rebels set up a powerful generator. They didn't believe in doing things by half.

Maariya   Just what I keep telling him. Look after your soldiers. Let them have some creature comforts . . .

Baabu   Will her Royal Ladyship kindly shut up lest we try that very instrument between her royal dugs? Too much luxury – that's what weakens the soldier. Makes him useless for a fight. Sleep rough, eat and shit rough, is that makes good fighting machine.

Maariya   Pig!

Baabu   Sow! Cow! (*Cocks a finger.*) Pow! Pow!

Fatasimu   You ready to try this, your Highness?

Biibabae   What is it?

Fatasimu   We call it the – Truth Prod. (*Moving to insert the plug.*) One second while I plug it to the outlet. When I give the word, all you have to do is apply it to part of the wire mesh. All set, your Highness.

Biibabae *applies the prod. A flash. Prisoner lets out a yell and the cage quivers violently.* **Fatasimu** *already filming the scene.* **Tikim** *wakes up in confusion and flees, screaming.* **Maariya** *is enraptured.*

Maariya   Once more. Do it again. Do it again for Mummy.

Biibabae   He was so funny. Did you see how his neck suddenly stretched out?

Baabu   Like cock about to crow morning time – the boy get observing eyes in head.

Tutor   I promised I would make a genius of him your Majesty.

Baabu   The boy born a genius! He take after us, which is as it should be.

Tutor   Of course your Majesty, my sentiment exactly.

Maariya   Come on, little genius of my womb. (*Advances. Her air of menace appears directed as much at the prisoner as at the prince.*) Do it once more for Mummy! (*Obviously intimidated,* **Biibabae** *obeys. The prisoner lets out a shriek and the cage quivers violently.*) That's our lad, that's our royal blood.

Encouraged, and entering fully into the sport, **Biibabae** *applies the electric prod again and again, while* **Baabu** *hops up and down in manic excitement.* **Tikim** *tiptoes back, still somewhat groggy, tries to takes in what is happening and at the same time assume a pose of nonchalance.*

Baabu   He's genius, Lady Maariya. We given birth to a genius.

Maariya   And you are a poltroon. Stop, you precocious little devil. You're going to kill him and there'll be nothing left for interrogation, which I intend to handle myself. I know how to get the answers I need – just let me do it my way.

Biibabae (*stamping his feet in frustration*)   I want to play, I want to play.

Maariya   And so you shall my dear. To your heart's content. You mustn't overindulge yourself or you'll kill the goose that lays the golden egg. Look at the little prince, he doesn't even know what fun is still in store for him. You've only had a bit of foreplay and you're getting all excited. Wait till we've sat him down on the tip of a rhinoceros horn and then you'll hear the rebel pervert squeal with ecstasy.

Baabu (*grimaces. Sidling over to* **Tikim**)   This woman the real pervert. Get better use for rhinoceros horn but she wanting to ram it up some poor bastard shithole. .

Tikim (*still shaken*)   I thought we were under attack.

Baabu (*gestures*)   Hey, she talking of rhinoceros horn remind me – much safer we divide the booty, what you think?

Fatasimu *seen shifting his lens between the pair and the 'roast chicken' scene.*

Tikim   Sure, sure.

Baabu   Dig deep hole where the she-wolf can't find it.

Tikim   My sister? Very good thinking. (*About to slump back to rest.*)

Baabu   Now, now, now! While her mind all taken with torture of prisoner. Go and hide half the rhino horn. Soon these conquered kingdoms start offering their daughters to King Baabu for royal harem. Baabu must be traditional king. Means he must have the horn of plenty. Go take care of booty.

Tikim   Leave it to me, Bros Majesty. (*Staggering out.*)

Baabu   You hear me whistle, that mean she coming near. (**Tikim** *staggers off.*)

Maariya   Now let's see what the flying trapeze artist has to say for himself. (*Takes the prisoner's head and yanks it half way round.*) Hard way or easy way, I'll get the answer from you. Who is your paymaster, or more correctly, paymistress? Is it not the wife of Rajinda? Yes? Moriya, not so? What did that slut promise you? If you try to hide anything from me I'll have your testicles cut off and sent to her for keepsake . . .

Baabu (*keeping watch for* **Tikim**)   Moriya, Moriya! Look like no end in sight to rivalry between you and that woman. She gone. Her husband finish, deposed, finish. He harmless.

Maariya   She has children and she's ambitious. This spy is one of hers, I know it. She's funding the rebellion. She wants to stage a comeback. I'll get the truth out of this whinnying donkey . . . Confess! Is it not Moriya behind all the unrest? (*Prisoner's head slumps.*) Don't you dare pass out on me. I want a confession! Biibabae! Give him a short dose to wake him up.

Leaping to action, **Biibabae** *applies the prod to the cage. Spurt of blue flames but no sign of life.* **Fatasimu** *comes forward.*

Fatasimu   I think we've lost our prisoner, your Majesty.

Baabu (*shrugs*)   Boys will be boys. And a spouse is sometimes even worse. (*Starts a warning whistle to* **Tikim**.)

Scene Five

A camp in the forest. **Potipoo**, **Potiplum**, **Shoki** *and* **Kpoki**. **Rout** *by himself, looking crestfallen. Maps, snacks, drinks on an improvised trestle. A war council in progress.* **Potipoo** *reads a dispatch while the* **Messenger** *waits.*

Potipoo   Your brother was always headstrong. He has taken leave of absence from his command in the UN operations and is heading home.

Potiplum　Bravo, brother. I expected no less.

Potipoo　He's already in the country. Trying to find his way to join forces with us.

Rout　It's the shot in the arm we've been awaiting, General. Potiplan will provide the credibility we sorely lack.

Potipoo (*bristling*)　Meaning?

Rout　No offence, General, but the infusion of new blood, someone who has never associated with the *ancien régime* in any way, that's what the people are waiting for. He has the reputation of an out-and-out professional. (*His spirits obviously rising.*) Citations galore in international peacekeeping operations. Never been guilty of ideological contamination.

Potiplum　I think you should choose your words more carefully Comrade Rout. The moment is not too far off when we shall test your own credibility.

Rout　I don't quite understand, Colonel.

Potiplum　You brought us assurance that the people are ready to rise. If we don't see any uprising when we move . . .

Rout　The people are ready. The workers are on the move. The petroleum workers will blow up the pipes and provide a wall of fire to consume Baabu's forces. You shall witness a popular uprising that will go down in history books.

Shoki　Every uprising so far has ended in Baabu's favour. He has exacted terrible reprisals.

Kpoki　Sometimes I wonder whether we're dealing with a human being or the Devil incarnate.

Potipoo　I always suspected he was not quite right up there, you know.

Kpoki　Then why did you keep advancing him, General. You kept pushing him up the ranks, way above his seniors and evident superiors. Now we're reaping the bitter fruits.

Potipoo Don't! This is no time for 'I told you so'.

Potiplum And it's not as if you didn't have a hand in the mess in which we've landed. You made the broadcast after all.

Shoki He had no choice. He had a gun to his head. We all did.

Potiplum I have still to be persuaded that you did not write the broadcast speech yourself!

Rout (*glumly*) No, he didn't write it. It was Tikim. I know, because I made some input into it. I put the ideological meat around the bone. You can shoot me if you like. (*Tears open his shirt and bares his chest.*) Here I stand. An ideological deviant deserves the worst.

Potipoo You? Comrade Rout? Why on earth . . . ?

Rout You have to understand. There are moments in history when revolutionary options within the dialectical process of the class struggle become severely limited. In this case, we were down to two – Audit or Sod it. Since you had refused to audit . . .

Potipoo (*wearily*) It was time to sod it.

Rout It was a gross misreading of the historic forces at work, nothing less than bourgeois deviationism and criminal adventurism. I am not afraid of self-criticism and I submit myself, if needed, to revolutionary justice. But the monster is loose, the monster that my unbelievable *naïveté* and dislocated patriotism has helped to create. I have tried to make amends. I have mobilized the proletariat for the final onslaught on the monster. This alliance between the suffering masses, workers and peasants and the progressive intellectuals will lead to a definitive installation of the dictatorship of the proletariat and the end of militarist interventionism.

Potipoo (*to* **Potiplum**) Does that mean he's now on our side?

Potiplum   He's here. He found his way here.

Rout   Our alliance is an alliance of common purpose. I wish to make it clear that the workers will not abandon their dialectical destiny.

Potipoo   I hope some of that means that he knows we either swim or sink together.

Shoki   We shall need a speechwriter. He's had some experience.

Guard (*off*)   Who goes there?

Rent (*off*)   Don't shoot, Don't shoot! We're unarmed.

Guard (*off*)   Advance and be recognized.

Rent (*off*)   I am President of the Royal Estates Nominal and Traditional.

Dope (*off*)   And I represent the Divine Order of Prelates Ecumenical. We come in peace.

Guard *ushers in* **Dope** *and* **Rent**.

Potipoo   So? My Lord of the Divine Order.

Dope   Your humble servant, General.

Potipoo   And my trusted adviser Royal Estates. (**Rent** *bows*.) To what do we owe this pleasure? I am sorry that I cannot receive you in the style to which you are accustomed.

Rent   No condition is permanent.

Dope   Not even this.

Rent   We have seen the error of our ways.

Dope   And we are here to make amends.

Rent   Our people are groaning.

Dope   The heavens are weeping.

Rent   The earth is wailing.

Dope   The very stones are bleeding.

Rent   Our ancestors have spoken. Their anger is in the thunder.

Dope   Their lamentations are rains of fire.

Rent   Our shrines are desecrated.

Dope   Our women violated (*They exchange glances.*) Indeed, why hide it?

Rent   Quite. Why hide what is known to the entire nation? Even men and boys have not been spared.

Dope   Nor beasts.

Rent   There are perversions in this land, unheard of in the time of our forefathers.

Dope   The escaped beast of the Apocalypse is among us . . .

Potipoo   Yes yes yes, but what do you want? Why have you pursued us here, you who placed the crown on the head of the man you now call monster.

Dope   SOS! Save our souls. Could any message be clearer?

Rent   But you have to change tactics. You must stoop to conquer.

Dope   It's Baabu or us.

Sudden shouts. Shots. **Potiplum** *looks round wildly, seizes his father and attempts to drag him out while swinging his gun to cover the new arrivals.*

Rent   Could it be . . . ? Could he have reached here already?

Dope   Truly is it said that the Devil rides on the whirlwind.

Shoki   I'll secure the perimeter. (*Dashes out.*)

Kpoki (*snatching up his gun, follows*)   This time, I'll aim for his head.

Rout (*snatches up a loudhailer*)   Ideology is the firing pin for the trajectory of the mind. I shall take care of their political orientation.

Potipoo   Yes, you do that.

Rout   *A Lutta Continua*. Victory or death. (*Exits.*)

Potiplum   Now for you two bastards! You led him here.

Rent *and* **Dope**   Never! On the graves of our ancestors, never!

Potiplum   He followed you here – that makes you guilty.

Dope   No no no! You've misread the situation completely. We followed him. He led us to you.

Rent   Then we sneaked out of his camp to warn you.

Dope   And to offer you a plan. The only way out.

Potiplum   Traitors. Fifth columnists!

Dope   By all the deities in heaven and hell, I swear we have a plan. We have consulted the shades of all the prophets, and the result is the same. He wins. He continues to win. It is time to change tactics. Since he emerges victorious, you must conquer him through his victories.

Potipoo   Are you going to talk in riddles? If that's all . . . Potipoo?

Potiplum   Voodoo talk. We have not surrendered to Baabu. Are we now to surrender to voodoo?

Rent   All right. Shall we tell them?

Dope   Yes, we might as well. General, there is bad news. Your son has been captured.

Potipoo   Potiplan?

Rent   Yes. He was betrayed by one of Maariya's agents.
And Baabu is using him as a human shield, together with
women and children. They've tied him to a cannon which
they roll forward. Your soldiers cannot fire on women and
children. Or on him.

Potipoo   Potiplan? This calls for a change of plans.

Dope   It was thanks to the excitement over his capture
that we were able to walk out of the camp.

Potiplum   Potiplan captured?

Soldier (*bursting in*)   Dispatch from Brigadier Kpoki,
General. He asks permission to begin an orderly retreat.

Potipoo   What's going on?

Soldier   Total chaos. It was bad enough being faced with
a human shield – and I am sorry to say this, General, but
. . . your son is among them. Tied to a cannon.

Potipoo   We know that . . .

Soldier   What you don't know sir is that . . . you may not
believe it sir, but it looks as if all the creatures of hell have
been let loose. There are monsters fighting on their side.
Our men are fleeing in terror.

Potipoo   Shoot all deserters!

Guard   We've made examples. They prefer to face death
than be wedded to the bitches of hell. Those creatures are in
their wedding dress. The men are throwing down their guns
and fleeing in droves.

Dope   The gates of hell are open my general. Your
salvation lies only in retreat. Leave the rest to the powers of
light.

A shot rings out. The **Soldier** *falls dead. A gigantic figure in full
wedding dress – a* gelede *masquerade adaptation – enters on stilts.*
(*Alternatively wheeled in on an improvised cart.*) **Dope** *and* **Rent**
dive flat on their faces, propel themselves out from under the tent. The

figure flings open its enormous skirt. Between the stilts is a man in uniform, shackled and gagged.

Potipoo   Don't shoot – it's Potiplan!

Potiplan   Oh my God! Come on, father. (*They flee.*)

Figure   After them my beauties, after them! After them, my avenging angels. Don't let them escape. It's shotgun wedding time in hell.

A column of hunchbacks and albinos, similarly attired, on stilts, stride swiftly across in pursuit, emitting firecrackers. Enter **Baabu**, *followed by* **Tikim** *and* **Fatasimu**. **Baabu** *makes straight for the food and drinks and begins to wolf them down. The* **Figure** *raises its veil – it's* **Tutor-Motivator**.

Baabu   Ha ha! It worked. I told you it would work.

Tikim   It was brilliant strategy, King Baabu.

Baabu   Nothing like a human shield, I telling you all the time. Take your hostages – especially women and children. And priests. Nobody shooting at priest. Too much fearing to go to hell.

Tikim   Even so, they did decimate a few of their civilians before they recognized Potiplan.

Baabu   I tell that stupid defector, Kpoki, but he arguing with me. Fine waste of money buying too many ammunitions. Make the enemy spend his own money on weapon, then use weapon to shoot down, blow up and otherwise eliminate his own loyal population. Is what I call military economics. Don't need to go to university for that.

Tutor   All hail King Baabu on yet another victory. Once again the enemy is routed. Long live King Baabu!

Crowd (*off*)   Long live King Baabu!

Tutor   Re-invent the continent!

Crowd (*off*)   Re-invent the continent!

Tutor-motivator *strides (or is rolled) out in the direction taken by* **Potipoo***'s group. A batch of women are pushed in by* **Bhieu***. They are very well endowed.*

Bhieu   We found these hidden in one of the tents, your Majesty. Shall we add them to the civilian prisoners for our human shield?

Baabu   Human shield? Has this Rapid Disposal portfolio gone to your head? Any more ideas like that and I relieve you of your duties. Oh yes, human shield, but special assignment. Hm. (*Brief inspection.*) Who are you? (*The women giggle, act coy.*) Ah, I think I like that kind of answer. No longer looking for that kind answer from my wife since many years, her mind far too busy on matters of money and power. Hm. So old Potipoo still at this game of slap and tickle, enh? Doing all right for himself I must say. Right. Take them back to royal tent. I coming soon to deploy them in person.

Women (*giggling*)   Long live King Baabu the Bountiful. (**Bhieu** *ushers them out.*)

Baabu   Ha! Seems to me they won't be needing much persuasion to cover royal corpus with their own bodies. Hey, you hearing those loyal prisoners? You hearing popular cry of people for their popular King? So you think you the heir presumptuous, enh? You sneak into country and you not knowing our royal consort Queen Maariya herself in charge of security. She and that master spy-catcher, Fatasimu. Think that department not placing royal spies all loyal to a thousand cuts all over the place, not to talk of Maariya's secret metamo forces watching and reporting subversive movement, following you moving and sneaking and plotting and recruiting and creating disloyalty and discontent? And you calling yourself international peacekeeper of United Nations, no? Oh, of course, can't speak yet, I see. (*Rips off the gag from the prisoner's mouth.*) Now talk!

Potiplan (*winces, recovers quickly and gathers up his dignity*)   I am on leave of absence from the United Nations peacekeeping mission. You have my papers of accreditation and I advise you to get in touch with my superiors in New York. By arresting me, you are taking on the United Nations. I would advise you against it.

Tikim   And his Majesty is telling you that you have no status in the kingdom of Baabu. You mean you haven't yet got that into your head?

Potiplan   In that case, I have nothing more to say. Do what you wish and face the consequences.

Baabu   Take him away. Tie him to one tree and I come do some practice shooting on him after we have small snack of victory.

Tikim   Your Majesty, I think I have better idea?

Baabu   Yes Tikim, Majesty always ready to listen.

Tikim   Ransom, your Majesty, heavy ransom.

Baabu (*reflects*)   Ransom? But his father on the run. Without money or anything to pay ransom. I think he broke as a church rat.

Tikim   The United Nations, King Baabu. I think the United Nations will pay to get back their man. I know how their minds work, your Majesty.

Baabu   Hn-hn? You mean the United Nations get interest in this common rebel?

Tikim   It's a matter of honour for them. I can travel rightaway and begin the negotiations.

Baabu (*face lights up*)   You know Tikim, you really good at thinking up profit idea. Foolish United Nations force still keeping control of the diamond fields next door where heavy fighting taking place. So now we tell them, pay our Royal Majesty full weight of Potiplan in basket of diamonds and we give you your man. Is good bargain I'm thinking, especially as rhinoceros horn not bringing in so much revenue these days. (*Giggles.*) Got better use for scarce rhino tusk, eh, Tikim?

Tikim   You've hit it as usual, your Majesty. They can have Potiplan against his weight in diamonds.

Baabu   Agreed. Prepare letter right away and tell them if diamond not coming back with courier, we start sending back Potiplan bit by bit.

Tikim (*fishing out writing materials*)   We can send them one ear to start with, your Majesty.

Baabu   Then a finger.

Tikim   Then the other ear.

Baabu   And then one finger. (*Holding up his hand.*)

Tikim   Maybe a toe, just to remind them we have plenty of bargaining points.

Baabu   And then we change to nipple. Pluck out one nipple, I think they knowing then we mean serious business.

Tikim   When we get to nipples they must capitulate. That should really put the squeeze on them.

Maariya (*crashes in, followed by* **Fatasimu**, **Biibabae** *and entourage*)   I heard that, you degenerate whoresons. Where is she?

Baabu   Oh Shokoriko, protector of greatness, how come this amazoness now barging in?

Maariya (*looking everywhere and overturning tables and chairs*) Where are you hiding her? You're supposed to be conducting a war to save your throne but all you're doing is playing with nipples. I heard you. I heard you with my own ears. Nipples, nipples, when you should be making war plans. TK, you drunken pimp, call yourself my brother but it's you leading my husband astray, supplying him with camp followers.

Tikim   Come on sis, he's not your husband. He is
husband to the whole land. He is King.

Maariya   And you are – Pimp!

Baabu   We recollect our decision to leave you take care of
last rebel camp I overrun and interrogate prisoners, not so?
So how you find it so difficult to simply carry out approved
duties, enh?

Maariya   I have to keep my eye on the war chest.

Baabu (*lascivious*)   What this dry chest know about war
chest? (*Loud, but still leering.*) War chests in good robust
condition, keeping under guard. Tikim, you see with your
own eyes, not so?

Tikim   That's right. Several war chests, bursting at the
seams were taken under guard some moments ago. I give
you my word, dear sis, they did not look in the least
depleted.

Maariya   I've checked the strongbox for rhinoceros horns
– it's empty. I've told you they are strictly for sale. We need
the foreign exchange but you keep grinding them to powder
to give yourself cheap erection.

Baabu   You in no position to know anything right or
wrong with my erection these past ten years, I'm thinking.

Maariya   And that's the way it's going to stay. You don't
become great by mixing sex with power, but it's no use
preaching sense to you.

Baabu   You just stinking jealous because traditional king
must have many wives. We not European or American king
I keep telling you. More like oriental. You not know how
many wives King David and King Solomon keep? Baabu
the Bountiful got to beat all record, Jew, gentile, Mussulman
and our own traditional.

Maariya   You are a maniac. Totally out of control. It's
women, women and women, not to mention young boys

and other orifices I won't mention in decent company. As for you, Tikim, call yourself the architect of Baabu's dynasty? You're nothing but the architect of his doom! Think I don't know that you share in the bag of rhino powder he carries under his bulbous robes?

Tikim   Oh, really, sis . . .

Baabu   What I carry? What I carry except machine pistol with seven silver bullet. And I'm thinking I ought to put one through your head this minute instead I bandying word with this daily madness. (*Unbuckles his belt and lays it down. The silver bullets are outsize. Takes off robes.*) Here. (*She pounces on the robes and begins to search.*) Better you find this rhinoceros horn powder you talking about or I putting one rusty bullet through your brain – no silver for you, oh no. Your brain not deserving anything like silver bullet. (*She turns on him and begins to pat him down, roughly.* **Baabu** *giggles.*) You tickling me, woman.

Maariya (*stops dead. Gives him a long, puzzled look. Slowly*) You never used to be ticklish. All your tickle parts are of dry elephant hide – that's how it's always been since I first met you.

Baabu   So? Suddenly I begin tickle in my middle age. Never heard of mid-life change in man? I think you say you know so much of everything.

Maariya (*sighs*)   It must be the – rhinodisiac. You wasting all our foreign exchange so you can begin tickling in your old age? All right. It's war. I will not stand for economic sabotage. You wait and see if I don't send you tumbling down the hill of disgrace and disperse you in winds of wilderness. Right now, I'm going to search the whole camp.

Alarmed reaction from **Tikim** *but* **Baabu** *simply settles in his 'throne', seemingly carefree.*

Baabu   Sure, you go ahead and search every corner. In meantime your friend Moriya who cause all this trouble escaping through the forest.

Maariya (*stops dead*)   Who? Moriya was here?

Baabu   Who you think escape just now with Potipoo and
Potiplum? (*Points to dead* **Soldier**.) Thas her personal
bodyguard who die defending her with last breath, giving
her hot covering fire while she escape with Potipoo and son.
After deadly duel, I give him one between the eyes.

Maariya   Which way did they go?

Baabu (*points, indifferently*)   But don't worry. I already send
Rapid Disposal squad to hunt her down. You look like you
need some rest. Stay here and have a snack of imported
caviar.

Maariya   I want her myself. I want to rip into her eyes
with my fingers. I want her blood squirting all over my face
when I tear out her liver. Come on. (*Rushes out with her
entourage.*)

Tikim (*sigh of relief, then applause*)   You are too much, King
Baabu.

Baabu   Nothing like hint of red meat to send bloodhound
breaking world record. Tikim, make sure she gone. Don't
want her changing mind and sneaking back while royal
sceptre busy discharging its duty. (*Exit* **Tikim**.) But first, I
get some reinforcement.

*Takes out one silver bullet, weighs it in his hand, rejects it and takes
another. Shakes it against his ear, nods approval and unscrews it. Just
then,* **Bhieu** *enters, pushing an opulent looking prisoner.* **Baabu**
hastily covers up the container.

Baabu   Ha. Who dis?

Bhieu   The so-called elected Mayor of Batwere, your
Highness. You . . . er . . . promised him a cabinet position if
he surrendered the city without a fight.

Baabu   Your people voted you mayor, you said?

Batwere   I am only here as the expression of popular will,
your Majesty.

Baabu   Ah yes, ah yes. Hm, what you think, Bhieu?

Bhieu   I still think an example should be made, your Majesty. This business of holding elections without the authority of your Majesty. It means anyone can simply take the law into their own hands.

Baabu (*excitedly*)   Thas it, thas it. Taking the law into their own hands. Thas where the problem is, I'm thinking. Taking law in own hands, voting with own hands and so on and so forth. (*Beckons to* **Bhieu** *who approaches. Brief exchange. Beams broadly.*) Well, our friend Mr Mayor, King Baabu ready to show you the King knows how to keep bargain. And seeing today is day of absolute victory, I go further and declare general amnesty. Bhieu, go and announce to the people of Batwere our royal decision. Bring what left of the human shield so we can give them amnesty in person.

Mayor (*bursts into tears of relief*)   Your Royal Highness, may all the gods and our ancestors reward you. Some people warned that you would dishonour our agreement but I said, No, a king is monarch of his word. And now this magnanimity your Highness, a general amnesty . . . I am rendered speechless. Now we see that everything we heard about you was a lie. We . . . we . . . permit me, your Highness . . .

Rushes to **Baabu***, sinks to his knees and takes* **Baabu***'s foot and places it on his head.* **Baabu** *leans down suddenly and grasps the man by the elbow. He brings the arm slowly up and scrutinizes it thoroughly. Nods thoughtfully. Re-enter* **Tikim***.*

Baabu   Tikim, glad you coming back so soon. You catch up with her?

Tikim   She's headed out at full gallop. All the same, I've detailed some boys to follow her and make sure she doesn't spring any unpleasant surprise.

Baabu   Good good good. Now, see what we have here?

Tikim   Oh, him. You don't have to keep your promise to a rebel.

Baabu   Well, I'm thinking, Tikim. Maybe now is time to correct public image.

Tikim   I don't quite understand.

Baabu   Well, I just granting amnesty to the people of Batwere. General amnesty to everybody.

Tikim   Your Majesty!

Baabu   But got to make sure it don't happen again . . .

Mayor   It won't, it won't, your Majesty.

Baabu   We make sure it won't. You wait outside till Commander Bhieu bring your people, then you lead them to swear oath of loyalty to King Baabu in person. Man, woman and children. After that, everybody go in peace.

Mayor   I am obedient to the wishes of your Majesty. King Baabu, I am overwhelmed, simply overwhelmed. The people will remain your ever loyal subjects, your Majesty. (*Exits backwards, bowing and scraping.*)

Tikim   King Baabu, are you sure this is the right thing to do? Once a rebel, always a rebel.

Baabu   Tikim, Tikim, is taking law into own hands which cause the problem, so we remove the cause of problem and matter of rebellion settle once for all.

Tikim   You mean to let them escape punishment altogether?

Baabu   Royal decision taken. Something for you to use polishing our image when you address United Nations – you tell them how our government grant general amnesty. (*Some movement behind the tent which is now lit up, so that we see the next action in silhouette.*) Ah, I think Commander Bhieu setting up the altar for oath of loyalty to our royal person. Once that taken, no more voting possible or taking law into own hands. And no chance of aiming offensive weapon at our royal person and loyal subjects.

In silhouette, we see a chopping block with two figures on either side and a huge basket on one side. The people of **Batwere** *are being lined up – men and women, the aged and children – covered by* **Baabu**'s *gun-totting soldiers.* **Baabu** *watches as each victim's arm is forced across the block and the machete goes up and down. Mouths open in a succession of soundless screams.*

Tikim (*clapping*)   Again you fooled me Bros Baabu.

Baabu   Getting fed up with trussed chicken and other forms of friendly dialogue. Think up that new variation on toilet seat this morning.

Unscrews the container and tilts some powder in his palm. Inhales from either nostril. Places some more on his tongue like snuff. Rubs some behind the ears and carefully screws back the cartridge, increasingly ecstatic as he watches the amputations.

This, and that – sight of it making double stimulation, no question. (*Tosses him the capsule.*) Time to go putting it to test on our first prisoners. Help yourself from silver bullet.

Tikim   Your Majesty is most generous.

Baabu   Get more fun hearing groans of pleasure right, left and centre. Same thing in battle. Groans in bed not really different from groans coming from amnesty, eh?

Tikim   I have had more fun in your Majesty's company these past months than I've ever had in all my life. Every day is an adventure. Long live my brother-in-law. Long live King Baabu!

Measures out a small portion and licks it. **Baabu** *watches him keenly, uneasy until* **Tikim** *returns the capsule. The amputations continue, rhythmically, ritualistically. As a basket fills up, it is replaced.*

Baabu (*taps the cartridge*)   Clever, though I say it myself.
That nosy consort of ours never think of looking for rhino
powder inside bullet.

Tikim   Indeed, King Baabu. The world will soon
recognize that Guatu is ruled by sheer genius. A master of
detail.

Baabu *turns slowly to watch the amputations. At each silent scream
his face expands with mounting ecstasy. Speaks as he exits backwards,
so as to keep his eyes on the scene to the last moment.*

Baabu   I feel the snake stirring in the bush.

Tikim   The sun is rising, your Majesty.

Basha   I hear the war-drums, they beating in my groin.

Tikim   The enemy lie prostrate at your feet.

Basha   We going to rip through them like devil of
firebrand, eh?

Tikim   The war-chests are open, they await your
Majesty's inspection.

Basha   Then what we waiting for? To battle! (*Spins round,
exits, followed by* **Tikim**.)

Light fades over amputations. Re-enter **Maariya** *with entourage,
minus* **Biibabae***, some wounded, including* **Fatasimu** *looking the
worse for wear. She is herself looking somewhat battered. Foul mood.
She becomes all the more furious on seeing the empty tent.*

Maariya (*to* **Guard**)   Where's the King?

Guard   The King did not inform us of his movements,
madam.

*She barely contains her rage, raises her arm as if she wants to strike
him, changes her mind. Sinks into* **Baabu***'s vacated seat.*

Maariya   Ambushed! Ambushed twice over. And the heir
apparent taken prisoner. My one and only son. Fatasimu,
how could you let this happen?

Fatasimu   Your ladyship, if you recall, I advised against following them into that plantation. It was a perfect setting for a trap.

Maariya   Did Baabu know? Did he send me deliberately into that trap? Sure, he was trying to get rid of me but – permanently? No, he wouldn't dare. Still, I never thought I'd see the day Sauna Bath would make a fool of me. Send me on a wild-goose chase so he can tickle some nipples. And my own brother aiding and abetting, setting up orgies and turning the palace into a brothel. (*Leaps up suddenly and strikes the* **Guard**.) I asked you where the King went. Where do they hold their orgies!?

Guard   Madam, I know nothing.

Maariya   Fatasimu!

Fatasimu   My pleasure, your Excellency. (*He disarms the* **Guard** *in a practised move and starts working him over.*)

Guard   I swear I know nothing. Madam, please . . .

Maraiya   You'd better speak if you don't want to see your testicles rammed down your throat.

Guard (*eyes suddenly widen in shock*)   The K-k-k-king.

Maariya   Yes, the King, where is he? My son is a prisoner, so don't think I have any time to waste on you. We must do a swap you hear? My Biibabae for their Potiplan. Better find your tongue before I cut it off . . .

Guard (*pointing a shaky finger offstage*)   It's . . . him . . . him, his Royal Majesty . . .

Maariya   Yes? Come out with it! Where has he gone?

Enter **Baabu**, *half-naked, a robe around his shoulders, feet dragging along the ground, supported by* **Tikim**. *His eyes are bulging, his tongue hangs out and he clutches his throat.*

Maariya   What's this? Pull yourself together at once! Is this a time for this sort of clowning? Your heir apparent has been taken prisoner!

Tikim   I think he's overdosed.

Maariya   Overdosed? On what?

Tikim (*helping him on to the chair*)   On what? He … . I have no idea. The first thing I knew, he was clutching his throat. (*A movement by* **Baabu** *lets the robe slip, revealing he is naked.*)

Maariya   What a disgusting sight – cover it up, Tikim! (*Walks away.*) What affliction from the winds of wilderness has overtaken him?

Tikim (*bends over to pick up the robe*)   It all happened suddenly. (*As he is about to rise, he stops suddenly, clutches at his throat.*) Oh? I . . . I . . . oh my throat, my throat . . . (*He snaps upright, stares wildly. Staggers forward.*) It's like . . . it's on fire . . . (*His eyes bulge. He runs towards the snacks trestle and gulps down some water. Breathes heavily, and appears to recover. Suddenly his eyes dilate with suspicion. He leaps on the cartridge belt and, with difficulty, extracts the silver bullet and unscrews it. Sniffs. His mouth opens wide and he stammers.*) Someone's . . . tampered . . . with it . . . !

Maariya   Tampered with what?

Enter **Rent** *and* **Dope**.

Rent (*ponderously*)   Tampered with Nature.

Maariya   Who? What are you . . . ?

Rent (*pointing. Same manner*)   The crown itself. When the crown is conjoined in the union of woman and beast . . . End of *Pax Baabunia!*

Tikim   Pax . . . pox . . . I tell you someone doctored this . . . this . . . this is not . . . not . . . the rhino powder. Someone has . . .

Rent (*indicating* **Tikim**'*s hand, preacher tone*)   It has happened as was foretold. Remember the words of the

Marabout? You were present. You declared it the coming of *Pax Baboonia*. It all adds up. (*Demonstrating.*) The horn of the beast hath penetrated the flesh of woman, in powdered form – through the royal sceptre.

Dope   Even so was it prophesied. Even so fulfilled.

Tikim (*sinking slowly, shaking his head in belief, shaky finger pointed at the pair, he moves towards them. The cartridge drops. He collapses on* **Baabu**)   You . . . you . . .

Baabu's *head falls on his chest. He is dead.* **Maariya** *screams.* **Rent** *and* **Dope** *look at each other, roll sanctimonious eyes skywards.*

Maariya (*slow welling up of hysterical laughter*)   He fooled me again. That goat-fucking degenerate, if he didn't fool me all along with that silver bullet of his. Who would have thought he was capable of having the last laugh. (*Sobers up suddenly.*) Last laugh? Last laugh? Shei-ge! The silver bullet did for him after all. Wait! He can't be really gone, is he? TK, do something, wake him up! Your dynastic edifice is crumbling. (*At this point,* **Tikim** *slumps, dead.*) What? You too? No, not both at once. Hey, my Sauna Bath, wake up, wake up! Potipoo and Sons Limited are out in the field, counter-attacking, you hear? We nearly fell into their hands but they took your son and heir apparent prisoner. You hear me, Biibabae has been taken prisoner! So if you die there is going to be problem with succession. Wake up, you hear me, wake up!

Brief commotion outside. Shots. Enter **Potiplum** *and* **Potipoo**, *followed by* **Shoki** *and* **Kpoki**, *and* **Rout**, *and a* **Guard** *leading* **Tutor-Motivator** *and* **Bhieu** *by a rope tied to their wrists.* **Fatasimu** *slowly backs against the wall. All stare silently at the tableau.*

Maariya   I see. The vultures are already gathering and Baabu not yet cold on his throne.

Potipoo   What happened here?

Bhieu (*a feeble salute*) I don't know sir. But I wish to make a statement. I was only carrying out orders. I'm only a small cog in the machine. I treated all prisoners like my own family. I loved them like my own brothers and sisters . . .

Fatasimu (*begins to pull out tapes and video cassettes from his pockets and brandishes them*) I have everything on record. I have the lowdown on everyone. I hold plenty of secrets. I can expose them all. I'll reveal everything – I'm sure we can strike a deal. I am strictly professional . . . you will always need my services.

Potiplum Why don't I simply shoot them out of hand?

Fatasimu *and* **Bhieu** *are roughly bundled out, one bawling 'Just a cog in the machine. One happy family' , the other 'Revelations! Amnesty! We can make a deal' and waving a cassette aloft until out of sight and hearing.*

Potiplan Can someone tell us what actually happened here?

Rent A prophesy fulfilled, nothing more.

Dope (*solemnly*) Heaven helps those who help themselves.

Potipoo (*disgustedly*) You'll get nothing but riddles from those two.

Maariya What have you done with my son?

Potiplan Escort the lady out. Take her back to her village. (**Guard** *moves forward*.)

Maariya Don't you dare touch me! (*Appealing.*) General Potipoo . . . (*He turns his back to her.*) Oh, so that's the way it is? (*Spins round with sudden ferocity.*) And what are you all looking at? You think this is a freak show do you? Well, don't you dare think it's over, oh no, by no means. It's much too soon to crow. I know you're going to start lying to the people, lying, lying, lying, you fake redeemers. You want to settle accounts but your accounts are safely stashed away you know where. And so do I. Now he's gone you'll all become butter-won't-melt-in-your-mouths latter-day saints. No, of course you never knew him, you never embraced him or sucked up to him, never used him when it suited you, you lying sycophants you stinking collaborators, you slimy accomplices . . . lying, lying, lying with your sanctimonious denials laundering your past so you continue without shame in the public eye, shameless, shameless, shameless, yes you kidnappers, torturers, murderers, of course now it was he who did it all, single-handed, no help from anyone, you never knew anything, just like the three brass monkeys, see no evil, speak no evil, hear no evil just pour stinking petroleum on the flames so you'll be sure to keep going on and on and on like the battery in the commercial with your little tin drum oh yes you know how to renew yourselves so people begin to wonder if their memory has failed them, if you're not the same people who drove them into the winds of wilderness but oh yes you'll keep going and going and going on and on and on . . .

As the lights dim slowly.